PRAISE FOR 7 *UNTOLD*
PROSPERITY AND LEGACY

"I see the vision and support the movement to close the wealth gap! This book has great ideas about shifting mindsets and redirecting our spend to also support entrepreneurship, ensuring Black business success, and creating business role models. Pick up a copy for yourself and someone you care about!"

—**Ron Busby**, President and CEO, U.S. Black Chambers, Inc.

"**This is a must read.** Homeownership is one of the keys to building legacy and intergenerational wealth. Eugene boldly and rightly connects the dots between growing the rate of black homeownership and closing the racial wealth gap in the U.S. This book is a must read for elected and government officials, business, civic, and faith leaders."

—**Antoine M. Thompson**, National Executive Director, National Association of Real Estate Brokers and Former New York State Senator

"**This could be the guiding book for the Association of Black Estate Planning Professionals (ABEPP).** *Closing the Racial Wealth Gap – 7 Untold Rules for Black Prosperity and Legacy* captures the strategy for creating, protecting, and transferring wealth. As estate planning attorneys, we are excited that this book shares the truth about the multipronged approach necessary for closing the wealth gap. We are clearly better together! Thanks, Eugene, for laying it out so clearly."

—**Aimee D. Griffin**, Esq., Managing Attorney, The Griffin Firm, PLLC and Founder, Association of Black Estate Planning Professionals

"**A WOW Book!!!** While many people think that you need a degree from a top-rated business school to learn wealth creation, Eugene has written a book that is a fast-read and easy to comprehend for everyone. This book shares simple steps to long-term financial success. It should be required reading!"

—**Dr. Willie Jolley**, Sirius XM Radio Host and Bestselling Author

"**This book has so many priceless nuggets.** Eugene's attitude and vision is contagious, and has profound ripple effects. In order to build intergenerational wealth, his book mandates this call to action: transition from ME to MOVEMENT!"

—**Maggie Anderson**, CEO, The Economic Empowerment Foundation and Critically Acclaimed Author

"**Let's move beyond the two C's!** With the teachings in this book, we in African American communities can move beyond the two C's at our celebration events and funerals—from, 'Who's bringing the Chicken and the Cake,' to, 'Who's bringing the Check!'"

—**Tony Hill**, Former Florida State Senator

"**This is a fantastic book!** *Closing the Racial Wealth Gap – 7 Untold Rules for Black Prosperity and Legacy* is a book to be enjoyed and learned from by people from all walks of life, no matter what your gender, age, socioeconomic background, or culture."

—**Ric Mathis**, Renowned Filmmaker, Black Friday Films Series

CLOSING THE RACIAL WEALTH GAP

CLOSING THE RACIAL WEALTH GAP

7 Untold Rules for Black Prosperity and Legacy

EUGENE MITCHELL

E. Mitchell Enterprises, LLC
New York

Published in the United States by E. Mitchell Enterprises, LLC

ISBN 978-0-578-45140-4 (*paperback*)
ISBN 978-0-692-97527-5 (*hardcover*)

For speaking engagements and book signings:
Visit: eugenemitchell.com
Or email: eugene@eugenemitchell.com

ACKNOWLEDGEMENTS

FOR MECCA: MY sweetheart and soul mate. Thank you for your unwavering support and encouragement; for bringing calm to the storm; for bringing strength to what is vulnerable; and for helping to navigate the way to a more fulfilled and rewarding life that delivers on our true, God-given purpose. There's so much more to do, and I'm happy and blessed to do it with you!

SPECIAL THANKS TO:

- **My Children and Blended Family—** Amir, Tatiana, Julien, and Jordyn. The four of you are lanterns in the darkness; you have inspired and enhanced my intention to make the world a better place for you.
- **My Parents and Grandparents—** Ambrose and Shirley Mitchell; James and Jesse Osborn; and Wilson Roberts and Agnes Mitchell-Roberts. You are all amazing, and exemplary role models for me. I am proud to bear, and carry on, your DNA.
- **My Sister—** Yvette Johnson. Thank you for always insisting on family love, big dreams, and living life to the fullest!
- **The $50B Dream Team and entire African American Market Unit—** You always believed in the vision, mission, and movement for us to create $50 billion in new Black wealth. And...we did it:

reaching our goal in 2017 after our seven-year campaign—*together.*

- **The Special $50B Believers and Advocates**— Tony Hill; Dr. George Fraser; Maggie Anderson; Nina Turner; Rev. Jesse L. Jackson, Sr.; Dr. Benjamin Chavis; and Mike Watson. I thank you for your endorsements, for lending your stature and credibility to making the dream a reality, and for blessing me with your incredible mentorship.
- **The Book Production Team**— Thanks to "Book Doctor" Petra E. Lewis for organizing and editing with excellence, Phil G. for the layout design, and Joe F. for proofreading. I also want to thank Todd Chapman for cover design and Candace R. McLaren for providing additional proofreading support.
- **Cirilo McSween**— To you and all those who paved the way, on whose shoulders I stand: As financial pioneers, and giants, you passed the baton to me, and I am paying it forward. Deepest gratitude to all of you. Your collective legacy lives on.

Thank you all for taking this journey with me to make this book possible, and for proving that ***together***...there's nothing we can't do. **Together, we know no bounds!**

TABLE OF CONTENTS

INTRODUCTION

IF WE EVER come together....

While talking to my good friend, Andrew, over a casual dinner in the fall of 2017, he shared a thought-provoking observation that he had made while watching the evening news: *He had seen diversity among the reporters get better over his lifetime, but the messages and images of Black people and the Black community get steadily worse.* What he shared led us to engage in a robust, hours-long conversation that ranged from the current, toxic political environment in Washington—including the intentional and corrosive rollback of Obama-era policies and decades of civil rights gains by the White House—to an exploration of the paralyzing statistics concerning Black wealth in the United States.

I shared with him the staggering projection I had heard: It will take 228 years for Black wealth to reach the current level of Whites' in the U.S. if we don't make radical changes in Black communities across the country. We discussed other studies, like the one that had recently come out in *The New York Times,* which found that Black boys, from even the wealthiest families, still earn significantly less in adulthood than White boys with similar backgrounds.

That conversation eventually evolved into an acknowledgment of the devastating and traumatic impact that the constant inundation of negative media images had long had on the Black community's psyche: depictions of violent crimes and arrests associated with Black people; scantily clad women; the glorification of conspicuous consumption that encourages young people to make a lifestyle of wayward shopping habits; and general images of poverty and despair—the sum total of which is meant to lead to broken families and broken spirits.

As our conversation began to wind down, we were both physically, intellectually, and emotionally exhausted. We sat in silence for several minutes. Eventually Andrew, who began to speak again, had moved on to lighter topics. I had not. The monumental weight of all the issues we had identified made it impossible for me to move, or to speak. Finally, overwhelmed by the enormity of my thoughts and feelings, I blurted out: "Man—could you imagine *if we ever come together?*" At that moment, it was less of a question, and more of an exasperated declaration. However, I immediately knew that I wasn't just speaking about our communities coming together, nationwide, in solidarity or to march in protest, but coming together spiritually, socially, collectively, and—most importantly—*economically.*

From that simple notion of Black unity—unity of purpose, unity of intellect, and unity of economic strength—I was compelled into action by the idea and promise of all that we could accomplish *if we ever come together.* With an absolute clarity that was both frightening and reassuring, inspirational and aspirational, I went home from that dinner, opened my journal, and began penning the contents of this book: a guide to fixing what ails us that was literally born out of the pain, anger, and frustration that has become commonplace for so many of us in the Black community. It's a mini-manifesto for the "woke folks" who know what is wrong, but oftentimes don't know what to do about it.

There's a legacy call and response in our community:

CALL

> *"If we ever come together..."*

RESPONSE

> *"...There is nothing we can't do!"*

We say this with confidence because we've *already* done it—and have seen the proof. By coming together, our ancestors helped to end slavery, win the right to vote, build institutions of higher learning and thriving towns, and force the hands of those in power to enact the civil rights legislation that made good on the constitutional rights that had been denied to us. In the twenty-first century, we need to come together again, with the same focus and singularity of purpose our forbearers showed in movements past—this time for enduring *economic empowerment.*

Fifty-plus years after the passage of the Civil Rights Act of 1964, we still have not achieved Dr. Martin Luther King, Jr.'s multifaceted call for change on all fronts. Many people only associate Dr. King's mission with civil rights, without realizing that, for some time before his death, he had begun to speak out against economic injustice. He expanded the demands of his platform to include equity in jobs and housing, and the dismantling of other institutional barriers that had disenfranchised Black people economically. For example, in 1962, Dr. King and the Southern Christian Leadership Conference (SCLC) launched what was known as Operation Breadbasket in Atlanta. According to The Martin Luther King, Jr. Research and Education Institute at Stanford:

> *[Operation] Breadbasket used the persuasive power of black ministers and the organizing strength of the churches to create economic opportunities in black communities. The group obtained employment statistics for industries selling their products in black communities and, if these statistics demonstrated that blacks were underemployed or restricted to menial positions, ministers from Operation Breadbasket asked the company to "negotiate a more equitable employment practice" (King, January 1967). If the company refused, clergy encouraged their parishioners to boycott selected products and picket businesses selling those products. By 1967 Atlanta's Breadbasket had negotiated jobs bringing a total of $25 million a year in new income to the black community.*

Dr. King's untimely death prohibited this part of his legacy from receiving the recognition or focus it deserves. That legacy is actually unfinished business. At the time of his death, Operation Breadbasket had only been rolled out in two cities: Atlanta and Chicago. One can only imagine the incredible strides that our communities could have made had economic justice for Black people, in addition to civil and social justice, been rolled out nationwide. This undertaking would have been preeminent in Dr. King's mark upon the world. We still have time to make Dr. King's economic vision a reality.

In order to facilitate real change today, just as we have done in the past, the Black community must show solidarity and unity to address the underlying issues of injustice and inequality. In prior movements, our ancestors had to stand for each other, or they would lose everything. Just like they did *then,* those of us who are able to now must take advantage of all available opportunities and information, so that we can come back and help the rest. This will require shared sacrifice, in order to yield shared community success.

The evening news has clearly shown us that we are not in a post-racial society, and that the topic of race is even more sensitive now than it has been in a long time. In fact, many of us have actually been slapped sober by so many of our civil rights gains being boldly and aggressively attacked. Some of us fear that we'll land at ground zero and have to fight the same fights our ancestors did, all over again. Many of us are also coming to realize that—regardless of our educational level, class, or accomplishments—we are even more closely tied together as members of the Black community in this current social and political climate, because of the color of our skin.

In being driven by the passion and concerns I just shared, I have two primary goals:

1. To teach you how to apply the tools, tips, and financial strategies to build wealth that have been withheld from us, or that we ignore, underutilize, or underleverage in the Black community; and

2. Provide insight, inspiration, and aspiration for others to join a NEW movement that is just as revolutionary and essential as the Civil Rights Movement, and is intended to bring about collective

economic empowerment, while closing the racial wealth gap here in America.

The moment is right for this movement to transform and elevate the Black community. We're not just focused on our $1.2 trillion of Black spending power; we're taking aim at the racial wealth gap—knowing that-long term, sustainable wealth creates opportunity, and the lack of wealth in our community continues to create hard times, desperation, and hopelessness. We are going to:

- Analyze the wealth gap;
- Look at tools to address the major components of this phenomenon;
- Understand what those with wealth do with it; as well as
- Focus on ways to empower individuals, families, businesses, organizations, and institutions to create a broadly thriving Black community.

I'll also share case studies of those who are already doing such work—and doing it well.

For those who are solely interested in "*What's in it for me?*," I advise you to put this book down, because its message is much BIGGER than that. There are lots of books that will talk to you about how to get rich, with the focus on *you*. This is not one of them. What I'm pushing for is a MOVEMENT, and I want to enroll soldiers, agents of change, and everyday folks.

If you are similarly fed up like Andrew and I am, angry about injustice and inequality, and ready to take a stand; push back; show pride; and be empowered socially, civically, intellectually, and financially: then this book is for YOU! Join us, and let's put a plan in motion, so that when our children look back 50 years from now, they will talk about this moment and movement. They will reflect upon our sacrifice and its impact on their current state of achievement, just as we harken back to the Civil

Rights Movement today. Let's work to ensure that MLK's entire dream is fully actualized, and that our future narrative on the evening news is one that speaks of positivity and promise.

Let's focus on what is collectively going to benefit US—as a community—together! Let's create wealth and legacies for our children, and for our children's children. Only... *If We Ever Come Together.*

We have no choice: No one else is coming to save us—***it's up to us.***

BLACK ECONOMIC EMPOWERMENT—PAST, PRESENT, AND FUTURE

THE OPPORTUNITY AND POSSIBILITY

I WHOLEHEARTEDLY BELIEVE that if we, **the more than 46 million Black people in America**, were to make better choices regarding where we spend our $1.2 trillion of annual earned income, so many things that currently seem impossible would become *possible*. We could:

- Eradicate poverty in our communities;
- Reduce our national unemployment rate;
- Decrease crime and eradicate the school-to-prison pipeline;
- Mend broken families;
- Lower incidents of divorce and domestic violence;
- Further academic or vocational pursuits and enhance existing public education;
- Increase overall home ownership;
- Reduce healthcare disparities among minorities and socioeconomically disenfranchised communities;
- Teach our children necessary money-management skills;
- Foster new businesses and entrepreneurialism;

- Build endowments to support and strengthen our organizations and institutions; and
- Galvanize and leverage social and political influence around issues impacting the Black community.

These are some of the opportunities and possibilities for our community that are born out of good financial stewardship and wealth management.

We have money, but what we actually *do* with it contributes to keeping us stagnant—or, in many cases, regressing—particularly intergenerationally. Our current, community-wide financial **ill**iteracy—wayward spending habits, lack of awareness, and failure to utilize the financial **Tools and Rules** that other races, religions, and ethnic groups have successfully implemented for centuries to build wealth—has resulted in glaring disparities for our families, businesses, organizations, and institutions.

Ultimately, this collective financial ignorance has prolonged our failure to close the racial wealth gap across this country. The outcome, according to the Economic Policy Institute (as of February 2017), is that the median figure for White wealth (i.e., family wealth that is exactly in the middle of the overall distribution curve) is *12 times higher* than median Black wealth. In addition, more than one in four Black households have *zero or a negative net worth*, compared to less than one in ten White families, and that gap gets even larger with time and age.

While I am specifically addressing U.S.-based people of African descent in this guidebook, what I'm about to share is equally applicable to all corners of the African Diaspora, as many in other countries didn't get to their tough economic state by themselves. Many of their financial challenges are due to similar political, social, and institutional racism in their parts of the world—in addition to the continued ripple effects of slavery.

So, what do we currently do with our money? Unfortunately, too many in our community have become wealth spenders—or, worse yet, wealth *pretenders,* in order to keep up with the proverbial Joneses—instead of wealth builders. Today, an alarming number of us are focused on accumulating products and symbols of wealth, rather than investing for the long term to build and multiply the cash we currently have. Some critics have actually referred to us as the world's greatest consumers—using our cash to provide us with instant gratification. It's important to understand that, while cash is fleeting, wealth is enduring.

Before going any further, let's take a minute to define economic wealth. Wealth is the difference between your financial assets (savings, stocks, bonds, mutual funds, real estate holdings, and money for retirement) and your liabilities (mortgages, loans, and debt). The amount remaining after this calculation is important, because it becomes a pool of cash that we can pull from to take advantage of opportunities and to adequately recover from emergencies. This reservoir (i.e., wealth) supplies the income stream for home purchases, college educations, and to begin and grow businesses. Those financial building blocks create even greater opportunities, and more wealth. If wealth opens the door to opportunities, conversely, the lack of wealth keeps doors closed—or closes open doors—creating a seemingly endless loop of challenges and hardship.

Oftentimes we believe that the key problems plaguing struggling Black communities are issues like crime, drugs, and single-parent households. These issues do, in fact, undermine our wealth and the power that it brings, but these problems are actually symptoms of a deeper-rooted, underlying issue. The true foundational problem at the heart of what ails our communities is *financial instability*, which leads to a lifetime of adversity and stagnation.

Even more disconcerting is that, in the 21st century, more than 150 years after emancipation from slavery, our communities have still not established nationwide financial stability; ongoing, autonomously driven economic opportunities; and multi-generational wealth for ourselves and our children. In short: *We are legally free, but still financially enslaved.*

> WE ARE LEGALLY FREE, BUT STILL FINANCIALLY ENSLAVED.

So, to put us on the right track to creating successful, thriving, and self-sustaining communities that contribute to the national well-being, we need an economic empowerment plan and a modern-day, wealth-focused movement to reroute our fiscal trajectory and change our financial future. A successful plan to accomplish this needs to focus on building, protecting, leveraging, and passing on foundational assets that foster opportunities, end disparities, and teach financial literacy and responsibility.

The plan would also need to focus on redirecting our collective $1.2 trillion in buying power toward strengthening the layers of our current infrastructural pyramid, comprising—from the bottom up—families, businesses, organizations and institutions, and overall communities. It would need to introduce some new concepts—widely used by other communities, but largely untapped by ours—for utilizing wealth-building financial tools and strategies. It would also have to address mindsets and spending habits in our communities, which we directly control. All of this would also need to be addressed within the context of the environmental and systemic challenges that our communities have faced for decades, and will, no doubt, continue to face for the foreseeable future.

The good news is that I've created the fundamentals of such a plan—with proven success in the billions—and a Black Wealth Movement of this magnitude is already underway! In my former corporate role, my team and I—in order to change the financial future of Black America—worked, since 2011, to build a modern-day financial movement. Our mission was to increase financial literacy in our communities and to redirect individual and collective spending toward the creation of wealth and the building of legacies. We embarked upon a wealth movement that stressed financial accountability and responsibility. We also taught, preached, and facilitated action based upon financial-planning information that has been highly underleveraged and often misunderstood in our community.

In my corporate-leadership position at one of the largest financial institutions in the world, with influence over the creation and distribution of billions of dollars through investments and insurance, I learned and gained experience in this area by watching what other communities were doing, how they were thinking, and what we have been missing. Using this knowledge, I founded the $50 Billion Empowerment Plan. My team and I worked with the 1,500 Black financial advisors and insurance agents at New York Life Insurance Company, along with dozens of business, community, political, academic, and press partners; faith leaders; and other institutions. Working together, we had a demonstrable impact on wealth creation in the Black community.

The vision was to expand and multiply what I had done for myself for others, using an underleveraged financial tool—life insurance policies—to build a collective $50 billion in wealth (200,000 black families x $250,000 of life insurance = $50 billion in financial security and tax-free future income) in five years. This amount is equivalent to the size of the total stock and value of General Motors (approximately $56 billion in 2017, including their plants, equipment, inventory, and buildings).

I'm happy to say that, in July 2017, we met our $50 billion goal, and were featured in several celebratory articles in publications such as *Black Enterprise, BlackPressUSA,* and other media outlets around the nation. Many of those articles included a photo of 250 campaign agents and ambassadors who joined us to stand on the steps of the Capitol building in Washington, DC. The varying captions read: "Milestone achieved and history made," and "50 years after the passing of the Civil Rights Act, a collective group of financial advisors have created $50 billion of wealth to continue empowering future generations in the Black community."

As you read this, that $50 billion is still active and benefitting the hundreds of thousands of Black families that are policyholders through this initiative for African-American communities. And this is only the beginning....

What we are seeing is an awakening of ambassadors who are sharing this message, a change in conversation, an encouraging reception, and a focus on the greater good for not only the Black community, but for all of America. Some are still doubtful and others too distracted or disconnected to recognize that there is no single greater issue facing our communities across America—regardless of race—than economic empowerment and financial stability.

I wrote this book to speak directly to individuals, families, financial advisors, and businesses about building solid personal economic-empowerment plans and tying them into larger community-empowerment initiatives, which everyone can participate in and benefit from.

How do I know this can work? Because, in addition to leading the agents and their clients, I have done it for my parents, myself, and my children—three generations of Mitchells, cloaked in financial security, thanks to these same financial methods. The future of the Mitchell family will be very different now. I have put the foundation in place, understanding that the results will not be immediate, but that, over the next 20–30 years, my children and grandchildren will be millionaires.

What's more, they will have the opportunity to use that inheritance to become multi-millionaires (who knows, maybe even billionaires!) and to create billions of dollars in collective wealth in the Black community. I am the one starting a new path for my family that has changed our legacy forever!

Building this initiative has not been without challenges or struggles, but the impact is already visible, and it is huge! Real talk: The naysayers, detractors, saboteurs, and haters have been busy *not* wanting to see success or Black wealth created; however, I am proud to say that we are doing it, and it is working! To that end, we will continue to spread the message and to work with those who *get* it—understanding that our financial health is part of the greater fabric of American wealth, and our country's place in the world. We want *every* citizen to see a brighter future.

WHERE WE ARE NOW

As of 2018, economic empowerment in the Black community reached record heights, with eleven Black billionaires in the world—as reported in the March edition of *Forbes* magazine—and several more in the making. We have witnessed significant progress in personal, business, and institutional economic successes, as well as growth to $1.2 trillion in earned income in Black America. However, if we make a comparison specifically to the family wealth of others around us, a substantial financial wealth gap still exists among those rosy statistics.

Since there are so many areas where we find ourselves operating on an uneven playing field (largely driven by race), to capitalize on all that America has to offer—at the same level and intensity as other communities—we must be financially on par with those communities. Otherwise, when it comes to our finances, we will have to exert far greater energy than these other communities simply to keep up.

The considerable analysis previously conducted on this wealth gap has provided perspective and insight. For me, a particularly important finding is that some children have totally different future outlooks and expectations primarily because of their families' financial positions. That finding touches so many of us in the African-American community, because of our persistent wealth gap. It also lets us know that we have made progress as a community but have not yet arrived; there is still work to be done.

Thus, to build a solid, numbers-oriented strategy to bridge this divide, I will use the racial wealth gap as the base metric to measure and track our continued Black economic empowerment. It is from this point of reference that we will define the contributing areas and current drivers of the wealth gap so that we can focus our activities to impact and positively change them. Let's explore this more.

According to the report, "The Ever-Growing Gap—Without Change, African-American and Latino Families Won't Match White Wealth for Centuries," by the Corporation for Enterprise Development and the Institute for Policy Studies, over the past 30 years, the average White family's household wealth has grown 85%, to $656,000. However, that of Blacks has climbed just 27%, to $85,000. That report, produced in August 2016, focused on average wealth, using data from the "Survey of Consumer Finance," which is published by the Federal Reserve Board in cooperation with the Department of the Treasury. It defined wealth as the value of assets—including a home or retirement savings—subtracted from the debt owed against those assets; and it excluded the value of durable goods like cars and electronics. At the time of that report, the gap between Black and White families was a whopping $571,000—a statistic that is expected to double to over $1 million by 2043 *if our community doesn't do something to change this trend's current growth rate.*

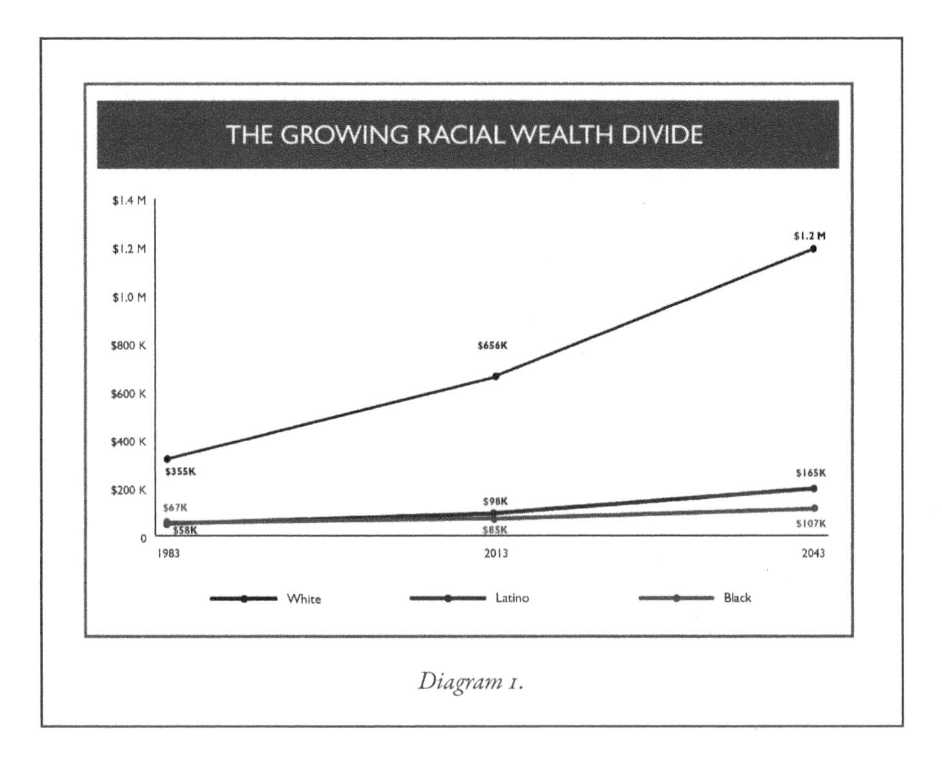

Diagram 1.

In fact, the report stated that—at the 2016 growth rate—it would take 228 years for Black families to match the average wealth reported for White families that year: $656,000.

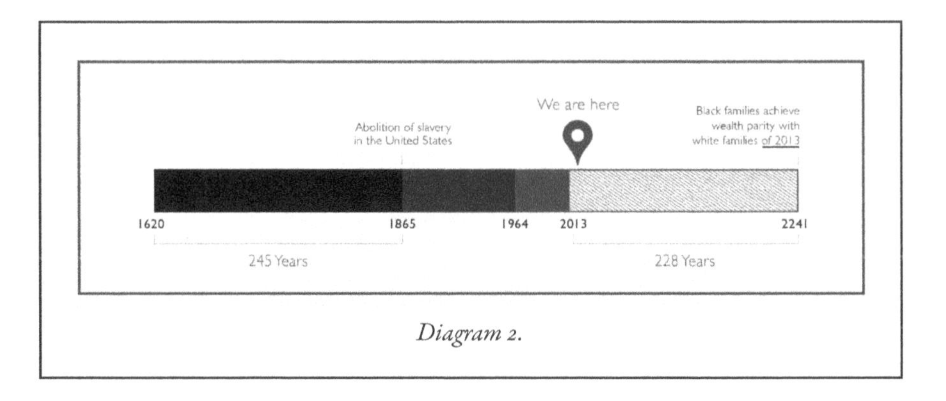

Diagram 2.

That means that when Black families actually *do* catch up to where White families were in 2016, those White families will have still outpaced and surpassed the wealth of those Black families. This constant state of lagging behind that constitutes the wealth gap will likely make African-Americans feel—even more than they do now—that they are *not part of the American Dream.* The wealth gap also affects our nation as a whole because those in poverty are often forced to rely more heavily on the country's social services. Of even greater concern to me is that, even though we know that other communities are doing better, our community is not *proactively* doing anything—en masse—to change this reality.

You should be as alarmed as I am—and I hope that you are!

HOW WE GOT HERE

MANY FACTORS—BOTH EXTERNAL and internal—have contributed to the disparity in wealth accumulation underpinning the racial wealth gap and the financial challenges currently found in too many parts of the African-American community. Some external factors include societal forces stemming from the impact of slavery, segregation, and long-standing institutional racism, as well as attacks on the Black middle class over the last few decades. Others stem from the many self-serving individuals, companies, and government entities outside of the Black community that profit from our lack of focus on, and knowledge of, how to manage our income and grow our assets and wealth.

The aspects of our financial predicament created by external factors—over which we have little, and sometimes no, control—gets further shrouded by our displaced responsibility and accountability. One can say that the Black community has been caught in an extended ***financial Jim Crow*** situation (separate and unequal) that some of us didn't even *realize* was happening. Remember: The most lethal lack of knowledge is *when you don't know what you don't know.* The end result is that the vast racial wealth gap between White and Black families, businesses, organizations, and institutions continues to widen.

Examining, once again, the timeline of the nearly 400-year Black experience in America (*See Diagram 2*), a more complete analysis of this situation shows that, for the first 250 years that African-Americans lived in the United States, the Black community accumulated no wealth because others reaped the economic benefits of their work, personal value, and control of their children's futures. For the next 100 years, Blacks were legally excluded from the financial tools and wealth-building strategies available to the general market, composed of White men and White families.

This only left African-Americans with access to their own newly created, inexperienced, and undercapitalized institutions. It is because of this that Randall Robinson, in his book *The Debt: What America Owes to Blacks* (2000), called for the United States to make reparations to African-Americans. He demanded compensation in the form of financial payments, as well as meaningful social programs and other solutions. Such reparations would atone for centuries of slavery, and for the imbalances, injustices, and discrimination that have continued to perpetuate the uneven playing field between Blacks and Whites.

In the more than 50 years since the passing of the Civil Rights Act of 1964, the Black community has tried to assimilate and embrace the benefits of integration, in order to build a strong financial footing for individuals, families, and regional communities. However, since that time there have been purposeful attacks on the Black middle class. These have included the introduction of laws and public policies—such as redlining and housing discrimination; discriminatory lending; restrictive insurance practices; and provisions in the tax code, like estate and inheritance taxes—that benefited wealthy Americans. Given the wealth gap, such affluent Americans were more likely to be White. In addition, most recently, the subprime loan crisis wreaked havoc on Black communities by allowing otherwise ineligible buyers to secure large mortgages—with variable interest rates and fluctuating, high-risk payment structures—that property owners were unable to sustain over time.

While, arguably, some of this predatory behavior was beyond our control, the impact and harm caused was compounded by the fact that we had not fully figured out the rules of the financial game—let alone how much to invest, where to spend our dollars, who to trust with our money, and long-term planning strategies to ensure intergenerational success.

Another factor contributing to the wealth-gap stemmed from the "War on Drugs" and its record-high increase in the number of incarcerated Black and Brown people. This "war" largely targeted poor urban communities of color, with increased law enforcement. It was a brand of criminal (in)justice that was often accompanied by mandatory-minimum sentencing and other punitive—often draconian, zero-tolerance—measures. The criminalization of what was essentially a public health crisis—the crack epidemic—also weakened and, in some cases, destroyed Black families. It robbed young Blacks of educational opportunities. It also disenfranchised people in our communities by denying them the right to actively participate in the democratic process once released from incarceration. Sum total: it was an era of crisis and despondency, plunging many of our communities into an economic spiral that has yet to fully end.

In spite of all these challenges, when you measure where we started, approximately 400 years ago, you have to give us credit: *We've come a long way!* Considering that we are hundreds of years behind with regard to financial literacy and money management, it's no wonder that we have subsequently reached varying degrees of individual and collective success in this country. The continuum of Black wealth ranges from abject poverty to Black billionaires, and from Watts (the once predominantly Black, low-income city in California that was first set back by riots in 1965) to Prince George's County (the affluent Black enclave in Maryland that is one of the richest African-American areas in the country today).

In the wake of intentional withholding of information and assets during slavery and segregation, and subsequent decades of discrimination, redlining, racially biased policies, and predatory schemes aimed at our communities, there has not been a *concerted* effort to properly educate and engage us financially. This is why our modern-day wealth movement and the utilization of the tools and rules for creating Black wealth are critical to getting us on track—and keeping us there!

In the midst of this chaos there have been people outside of our communities who have profited from our ongoing financial losses and misguided wealth spending. By adhering to this status quo—rather than challenging it—our enthusiastic participation in this paradigm has created an even greater negative impact on us in the areas of health, education, workforce development, and the legal system. The truth of this dawned

> WHY HAVE THE SECRETS TO CREATING AND PRESERVING WEALTH REMAINED UNTOLD TO US FOR SO LONG?

on me as I stopped to wonder: *Why have the secrets to creating and preserving wealth remained untold to us for so long?*

What has become abundantly clear to me is that there is big business and profit to be made by keeping the system this way—and keeping *us in the dark*. Simply told: There is huge revenue in ignorance. We are happily spending our wealth, instead of protecting, building, leveraging, and passing it on to future generations. Collectively, we are spending on what we can't afford, borrowing to acquire material goods, and paying inordinate amounts of interest to do so. Often our doing so is both by choice and by design—as there are those who are disinterested in seeing a strong, thriving, self-sustaining Black community emerge.

Corporations build out projections based on such reckless behaviors. Over the past 60 years, advertising executives have been rewarded for operating on the conclusion that Blacks buy brand names and expensive symbols of quality and prestige. *The Secret of Selling the Negro Market*, a 1954 film financed by Johnson Publishing Company, the original founder and owner of *Ebony* magazine, helped cement this approach to marketing to African-Americans. The film was originally intended to encourage advertisers to promote their products and services in African-American media at a time when Jim Crow segregation had begun unraveling (the Supreme Court's historic *Brown v. Board of Education* decision also happened that year). The reel was meant to emphasize the economic power of the Black community as a demographic. Having achieved its goal, however—in my opinion—one of the unintended ripple effects is that this brand of marketing by corporations has helped to condition us to consume—and to do so vigorously.

What is just considered to be benign capitalist ideology—an economic system based on production of goods and services for profit—has actually had a negative, and long-lasting impact on the Black community by siphoning much needed capital away from it. This has resulted in a dearth of resources and the demise of many Black businesses and institutions that have been unable to compete with the scale, sophistication, branding, and funding of outside competition.

In addition, the perpetuation of poverty has produced high-interest, predatory lenders—like check-cashing businesses that offer payday loans, and rent-to-own furnishing companies—that further financially weaken our communities. The costs connected to being poor—in fees and charges—as well as a lack of service and access to economic support structures are all too prevalent. As an example, some analysts cite a "poverty tax," where even items like standard grocery staples cost more in poor communities of color. Rev. Jesse Jackson, Jr. called it a "skin tax"—where Black people pay more to get less; work harder; and die sooner. We've been stuck in a money trap for hundreds of years, with no answers, no leadership, no destination, and seemingly no end in sight.

Now that we have explored some of the external forces that have exerted—and continue to exert—undue influence on our communities, it's also necessary to examine the internal forces that play a wealth-depleting role and stagnate our progress. Let's start here: *Our lack of understanding regarding our value and our worth has hampered our progress both economically and socially.* This lack of understanding also prevents us from working together for our collective benefit, which keeps us from trusting one another. Considering that no post-traumatic stress counseling or assistance followed hundreds of years of slavery and barbaric acts, it is going to take extra effort and time to rebuild families and reestablish strong, vibrant, foundational community pillars, such as two-parent families, education, wealth building, and intra-community trust. Similarly, internal factors related to personal decisions and actions, and their outcomes, have also hindered us. Add to that a lack of knowledge, fear, mistrust, and lowered expectations, and the gap has mushroomed.

This mindset persists today across our collective Black community, fueled by things like those in a lower income bracket feeling that they *just can't make it,* and that they don't believe that middle- and upper-income Blacks will come back to help them get a leg up. Even many of us who have "made it"—using annual salary as a yardstick—are the first in our families to earn six figures or more, and we sometimes feel pressured to *prove* our success. Some of us do so by parading around with symbols of wealth that we can't actually afford, instead of building up genuine, long-lasting wealth for ourselves and the next generation. Proverbs 13:22 says, *A good man leaves an inheritance to his children's children.* Nowhere does that verse talk about popping bottles in the VIP section of a Vegas lounge as part of a regular lifestyle.

I want to equally stress lapses in personal accountability and responsibility for our actions as additional examples of the internal forces affecting our wealth accumulation. These, coupled with displaced priorities and lowered expectations, are actually things that we can control and change. Unproductive cycles within some Black families, like continual reliance on government assistance, multiple siblings and generations in prison, and flat-out poor spending decisions, are forces that will challenge the wealth movement that we're trying to create together—and stand diametrically opposed to its positive message and influence.

It's understandable that, to a certain degree, rising above such circumstances as low self-worth and low expectations is not easy when those of us dealing with such social and financial pressures aren't aware of the time-proven financial tools and rules that exist. No one has taken time to educate and mentor many of us about them. However, we alone are responsible for—and have to rein in—the self-inflicted wounds of willful ignorance and a disinterest in seeking out such life-changing information. It's our lack of proactivity that, combined with external forces bent on doing us harm, continues to contribute to holding back some Black folks who are extremely talented. Look up. And for those of us who are asleep, wake up. The future is bright—if we *want it to be.*

RAISING OUR AWARENESS AND CONSCIOUSNESS

As a corrections officer at a maximum-security prison in Florida for four years, I was able to see, firsthand, that many of the issues we believe to be the true problems and detriments to the Black community are actually only symptoms. The usual suspects—crime, drugs, violence, single-parent households, the high school dropout rate, and teenage pregnancy—are actually outward, visible manifestations of more deeply rooted foundational problems. The real issues are a lack of money, educational and career opportunities, and sage financial and life guidance.

In recent years, the disconnect and frustration that are outgrowths of these issues have flared up in protests in cities such as Ferguson and Baltimore—fueled by incendiary acts of social injustice—as well as in past decades in cities like Newark and Watts. Even though we have reached political, social, and educational heights as individuals we still haven't developed the kind of community infrastructure needed to effectively address the underlying, modern-day issues in places like Ferguson and Baltimore. The reality here is that future injustices can ignite similar issues again like a powder keg.

This weak financial foundation not only affects us as individuals; it impacts our families, structures, businesses, organizations, and institutions. Consequently, many of our community pillars are broken and/or dysfunctional, without many credible ideas for rebuilding and restoring them. I believe that there is still a chance to fix them. To do so would include cycling enough of our dollars back into Black businesses to grow profits and jobs, and to raise up role models for others to follow. In short, we must coordinate our efforts to focus on building a strong economic power base.

HOW WE GET AHEAD

As the title of this book alludes to, in order to get ahead and achieve our maximum potential collectively, as a people, *we have to come together.* Not only must we have a mindset of growth, abundance, unity, and love, but we must also connect to what we know is working, disengage from what we know is *not* working, and rally around a movement designed for involvement by all. We have to have the strength—mentally, physically, and spiritually—to stay the course as we stand together. We must be prepared to fight the waves of resistance to our economic unity and progress, as well as the inevitable undertow of doubt, pessimism, and waning commitment that will make some of us feel like jumping ship when it comes to collectively creating change. We also have to soberly recognize that, along the way, *some of us will drop out.* To prepare for and deal with the inevitable challenges ahead, we should mentally prepare for this collective undertaking by focusing on the impact that we can make in the professions in which we are knowledgeable or have expertise, the community spaces that we know, and the financial tools that we have mastered—all to effect long-term economic change. Having this mindset will keep us motivated.

A central aspect of this movement is leveraging each other's expertise. So many of us are doing great things individually; we must now collaborate to exponentially multiply our efforts. To that end, I aim to accelerate such collaboration into action by adding my voice to the small, but growing, chorus of ambassadors for a community-wide wealth-building movement. This book will highlight people, programs, and businesses for you to unite with. For my part, I will shed light on the areas and financial tools that, based on my long career in financial services, I know can make a difference. I have an understanding of macroeconomics, and my approach to microeconomics is filtered through a historical and fiscal prism specifically related to us. My personal expertise centers around life insurance and financial planning.

After we come together, the next step is a concerted, collective effort to apply our specific areas of expertise to those areas in which we can have an impact in closing the wealth gap. For example, a school teacher can infuse financial guidance into his or her lesson plans; an attorney can be an advisor for a family's financial decisions—for instance, crafting a will; an elected official can be a supporter and advocate for small Black businesses, and so on. Anyone reading this book can help to make their individual dent based on their specific expertise. This is how we will structure a caring, concerned, and connected community with a long-term financial focus—ultimately building the savings, stability, and strategy for collective financial uplift.

What's exciting is that these efforts to address the wealth gap in our community have not been executed in this manner before. To have this specific intention and destination is to have *success.* Let's give some definition and detail to these wealth-gap areas, using findings from the article, "The Roots of the Widening Racial Wealth Gap: Explaining the Black-White Economic Divide," published by the Institute on Assets and Social Policy in February 2013. In it, researcher Thomas Shapiro and his colleagues show five key areas that are partly within our "locus of control" that, if we were to make significant strides in today, would likely make real progress toward closing the wealth gap in this generation, so it is not passed onto the next one. One area in particular that I want to emphasize is the creation and growth of the inheritance that we pass on to the next generation (and future ones).

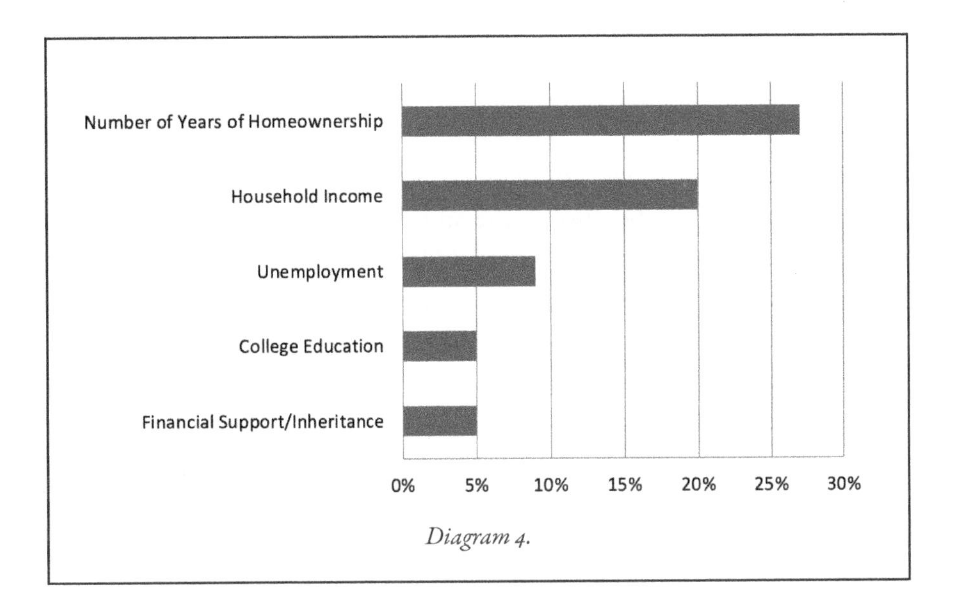

Diagram 4.

As shown in the diagram, the five major contributors to and current drivers of the growing racial wealth gap are:

1. Years of homeownership;
2. Household income;
3. Unemployment (more prevalent among African-American families);
4. Education level—specifically, being college educated or not; and
5. Inheritance, financial support by family or friends, and preexisting family wealth.

They also include the corresponding percentage increases to the wealth for White families, relative to African-American ones, which were studied over a 25-year period (1984–2009). The first and largest disparity between White and Black families is in the level of homeownership and years of ownership (27%). Helping to substantiate this finding is the overall homeownership rate provided in 2018 by the U.S. Census Bureau: 72.2% of Whites owned homes, versus 41.7% of African-Americans at the end of 2016. We must also recognize that home values appreciate differently in different neighborhoods, with much less growth occurring in Black communities, which adversely affects wealth building. These disparities point to our need to focus on home buying as a major wealth-building tool, in part because of the additional benefits of home ownership, like the ability to file a mortgage deduction on your income taxes. There's also the appreciation in your home's equity, and overall value.

In this book's Resources section, I've highlighted a powerful new program by the National Association of Real Estate Brokers (NAREB), the goal of which is to increase African-American home ownership by 2 million homes over the next five years. This program is an example of great work being done; we should all help to support and promote their effort to achieve this goal. This mission is not only designed to empower each individual family, but to have a collective impact. If we rally real estate agents, mortgage brokers, inspectors, contractors, and others to come together to leverage and promote each other's expertise in the area of home ownership, we can directly influence a major component of our growing wealth gap through our wealth-focused movement. The importance of homeownership cannot be overstated, so I will share more about this program, and others like it, later in this book. Let's make homeownership a primary focus.

For the next three areas highlighted in the study as contributors to the wealth gap—household income (20%), unemployment (9%), and education level (5%)—let's discuss them within the broader context of our community decisions around **health, lifestyle, and continuing education:**

Health—In our community we must acknowledge the serious expenses associated with African-Americans not maintaining good health. These include chronic illnesses, underlying genetic diseases like diabetes and hypertension, as well as obesity, lack of care, and poor eating and exercise habits. Each can have negative effects on our wealth accumulation by impacting our ability to work, as well as the number of years that we're able to work; the salaries that we're able to demand; and our ability to save those earnings. In short, the added expenses associated with healthcare impact our household incomes and impede our ability to build long-term wealth. When you think about it, economic loss is not usually associated with any conversation about health, but you generally have to be healthy to make money and to be able to invest and build wealth.

Longevity is the key to maximum earnings and to enjoying all of your days. Things like eating healthy, exercising, and getting regular medical checkups have to take priority. As someone who works in the insurance industry, I'm always shaken by the calculations of projected deaths based on high school reunion dates. For instance, according to an Insure.com article, titled, "High school reunion shocker: They're dying off!," out of a graduating class of 330, it's projected that three classmates will pass by the 10-year reunion, seven by 20-year reunion, 15 by 30-year reunion, 32 by 40-year reunion, and 70 by the 50-year reunion. I know that I'm trying *my* best to not be one of these statistics. Let's stay healthy—and make that money!

Lifestyle—When I think of the term *lifestyle* in the context of the racial wealth gap, I think of things that influence our social and economic progress, like joint-income households, single-mother birth rates, incarceration, and unemployment rates. The advantage of joint-income households is that combining earnings can help couples accumulate assets faster because it's easier to focus on wealth-building strategies and cost-saving actions when you are splitting bills. However, while couples living together can be a financial advantage, I also personally know all too well the stress of breaking apart.

Alimony and child-support payments not only mark the end of a two-income household through divorce, but a couple's split also inhibits the ability to expand the rate and pace of accumulated savings and investments that come from two people making conscientious financial decisions together. I once heard it said, "Marry the right person because that will decide 80% of your happiness or sadness in life." I say, when it comes to marriage and partnerships, this applies to your *financial* happiness in life, too!

Next, I want to note the unique dynamic in our community of 72% of babies being born out of wedlock. I'm only highlighting this to acknowledge the challenge of accumulating and retaining wealth without the foundation, contribution, and shared responsibility of a nuclear family unit. While bringing a child into this world is often a beautiful and joyous occasion, single parents must consider the social, emotional, and financial ramifications of raising a child in a non-nuclear household. I think we must share with our young people that, as single parents, they will have to make an extra effort to overcome the statistical, historical lag in wealth creation in order to get ahead in life.

In addition, the penal system—which has had a disproportionate effect on Black communities—also undermines wealth building. Whether it is jail, prison, parole, or the stigma of a prior criminal conviction, crime does not pay when it comes to trying to land a good-paying job. It also robs imprisoned members of our community of the time needed to accumulate wealth—time spent locked away in a cell, instead of as a free, income-earning citizen.

As a former prison guard, I want to stress to our young people that rappers and reality television shows that seem to gloss over stints in jail as no big deal at best, and as cool signs of street credibility at worst, is a falsehood that robs our youth of the future's many gifts.

Doing time in jail is neither glorious nor something to be proud of. Add in attorney fees, fines, and the cost of lost opportunities that comes from forgoing career options while incarcerated, and it becomes a major financial drain on individuals, their families, and their communities. Likewise, the higher unemployment rate in the Black community is also a wealth-creation issue. I encourage young people, especially young men, to focus on acquiring a skill, trade, or college education.

While we can't control whether or not we are offered a job we've applied for, we can control our job preparedness. We can also support Black-owned businesses that are more likely to hire other Blacks, by patronizing and utilizing their services to ensure their success. A great study conducted by my friend, author and activist Maggie Anderson, and The Levy Entrepreneurship Center at Northwestern University's Kellogg Graduate School of Management proved that we can create one million jobs in the Black community if we were to increase our household spend with Black-owned businesses from just 3% on average to 10% across the country. It's a virtuous cycle: Enhancing our skills allows us to build businesses and to hire others in our community—and such hiring increases Black employment, and our collective ability to save and invest. I discuss this concept in more depth in the Resources section.

Continuing Education—I know it's pretty self-explanatory, but, as our parents told us: *Education provides us with greater options.* Since our community faces particular challenges (like failing school systems), we must emphasize personal responsibility and accountability to stay in school, and to excel, with the goal of earning a good wage and accumulating wealth. In areas where the educational system is subpar, parents—and students themselves—must seek out free and low-cost tutoring and enrichment programs that balance out a school's inadequacies and keep our scholars on track.

EDUCATION PROVIDES US WITH GREATER OPTIONS.

Our high school dropout rate is not a score that we need to highlight, but we must fully understand the consequences, especially for young Black males, of dropping out of school when it comes to job opportunities and salary. As a young Black man growing up in Brooklyn, I, too, fell victim to peer pressure and being too cool to carry books or raise my hand in class for fear of being seen as a nerd. I recall being entranced by the trappings of short-shelf-life pursuits like clothes, sports, and chasing girls. I agree with the proverbial saying, "It takes a village to raise a child," and we must impose and embrace a sense of collective responsibility for our group success by demanding more from ourselves and each other. We must also imbue our youth with the weight of awesome expectations. No matter how much Black folks earn and how educated we become, the reality is that we cannot "pass down" our jobs or our fancy degrees to our children. Our accomplishments—in this context—are non-transferable, so an emphasis on education must continue for every generation.

This notion may be lost on some young people who believe that a college degree is no longer a prerequisite for future success. When they see college dropouts like Facebook Founder Mark Zuckerberg go on to become billionaires after deciding to leave college, those young people, who believe that academic credentials do not hold the weight that they once did, may feel like they're on to something. However, just remember that billionaires like Zuckerberg and Bill Gates dropped out of *Harvard*—not Never-Heard-of-It Community College.

On the flipside, perhaps inspired by the Obamas, college attendance rates for Black and Brown young people reached record highs in recent years. However, some of those same young people quickly became disenchanted by the burden of student loans without rosy job prospects after graduation. Nevertheless, educational attainment remains *extremely* important—and is closely tied to wealth creation. Higher education or advanced schooling provides more than additional academic rigor: The types of relationships that lead to both genuine friendships and strong professional networks often start in college and graduate school. Honing your critical-thinking skills, furthering your social maturation, expanding your worldview, and enhancing your cultural intelligence are often positive by-products of a higher-education experience. Holders of bachelors, master's, and doctoral degrees can then leverage these enhanced skills for future success and wealth creation.

For the last wealth-gap contributor highlighted in the Institute on Assets and Social Policy study—"Financial Support/Inheritance (5%)"—I want to lend my specific expertise. This area is where we can make significant progress in boosting wealth creation for the Black community to the tune of tens of billions of dollars in a relatively short amount of time. This is an area that has not traditionally been on the radar for us to leverage. Family inheritance encompasses more than simply money passed on at death. More broadly, for young adults, it often includes helping to pay for college, substantial down payment assistance when buying a first home, and other ongoing parental financial assistance until emerging adults gain firm financial footing. Many of us, as Black people, feel that it's a badge of honor for each new generation to pull itself up by its own bootstraps—to instill hard work and discipline. It's not. Being at a financial disadvantage is a hamstring, rather than bootstrap, and keeps us collectively stuck.

Many of the following sections of this book will explain family wealth-building strategies. One in particular I will take a few minutes now to begin to demystify in this realm of inheritance—and that it is how to truly and *properly* use life insurance within our families and the community to attain our wealth-gap objectives.

LIFE INSURANCE: AN UNTAPPED PATH TO BRIDGING THE WEALTH GAP

For some of us, it may seem like a misconception to talk about life insurance as a wealth-building tool, because most of us are only familiar with its role as something that *kicks in upon my death*. I challenge you to shift your thinking and embrace the LIFE in life insurance. In addition to creating security, benefits, and wealth for others upon your death, the acquisition of life insurance can help to protect YOU in the HERE and NOW—and enhance your quality of life. It can also help to birth your hopes and dreams into reality by safeguarding and underwriting money for:

1. Paying for college;
2. Purchasing property;
3. Funding retirement;
4. Providing a capital source for opening a business;
5. Delivering investment guarantees and tax advantages; and
6. Enabling you to create an instant estate.

Inheritance through life insurance is something that we can control, based on the amount of the policy we purchase and that we keep our payments current. It can also create wealth where there was none before. With a $500,000 life insurance policy being paid out at some point in the future, a family can bridge the wealth gap in one generation and may actually be able to get ahead of the curve if its members were to take out more insurance. In addition, we will discuss how you can borrow against the cash value built up from the semi-compulsory savings in permanent policies, to lend a hand in paying for college or to secure a down payment for a home purchase while the insured person is alive. (These terms will be explained in more detail in Rule #2 of the 7 rules comprising the "Untold Rules for Black Prosperity and Legacy.")

The next part to the life insurance story, of course, is the death benefit. It is the amount that will be passed down through the policy and, if positioned properly, can help children and grandchildren move beyond incremental financial strides forward, and, instead, leapfrog ahead to a position that is commensurate with their White counterparts. This concept can make true, broad-based generational, societal, and community change. In Rule #2, I will deliver more ideas, tips, and suggestions on how we can take advantage of life insurance's full potential.

A more sophisticated approach to structuring and capitalizing on life insurance can counter—and even cure—some of the most destructive manifestations of our low self-worth and lack of investment in our own legacies, businesses, neighborhoods, and institutions. However, from my experience, I have discovered that it is a harmful combination of deliberate misinformation, factual omissions (on the part of the life-insurance industry), and our own self-defeating thinking and misguided actions that have kept us from using life insurance to build wealth. Let's examine those three areas I've touched upon more in depth, under the umbrellas of: Information Omitted, Action Committed, and The Enemy Within (the latter being self-defeating behaviors in our community).

THREE KEY STUMBLING BLOCKS TO BLACK WEALTH

Since starting my career in the life insurance industry in 2001, I've been uniquely positioned to observe detrimental overt and covert actions by the individuals and companies that were supposed to serve us. This mistreatment resulted in the miseducation of African-Americans with respect to the benefits of life insurance, and in a loss of trust in the industry among those in the Black community. The cumulative impact to our financial progress has been vast. Let's first take a deeper look into two categories: "Information Omitted" and "Action Committed."

Information Omitted

Over the past 150 years, for many in the Black community, insurance companies and agents have messaged life insurance almost exclusively as a tool used to pay for the cost of someone's burial. However, in many cases, for those who took out basic burial policies, their checks didn't even cover those expenses. This practice started with the benevolent societies after slavery. It then evolved into the industrial policies that debit agents from large and small companies sold door-to-door in the Black community (often for only a few pennies and dollars at a time), and it continued with Black-owned insurance companies during segregation.

These agents told members of a family, particularly matriarchs like the proverbial "Big Momma," that by buying such basic burial policies, they'd be able to have honorable funerals with no burdens posed to their loved ones upon their deaths. So many in our communities willingly took small policies out on themselves—and on all of their children, to avoid the shame and humiliation of a pauper's funeral. No one had ever truly talked to these policyholders about insuring for a greater value—let alone the possibility of creating a legacy by which they could be remembered or providing a hand up to others in their families. In addition, Big Momma's financial contribution to the family may have been $20,000 a year, and her funeral may have cost $5,000. Little did they realize that policies that covered the funerals, and not the head of household's lost income contribution to the family, were actually of little to no use.

I've noticed that since life insurance is not mandatory—unlike car insurance or mortgage insurance—life insurance firms do not affirmatively promote it as a standard topic of conversation to most Black households. It is not positioned as a necessary instrument for income protection, and, in some cases, not even for a bare-bones burial. As a result, this lack of knowledge has left many in our community content to just go without life insurance, or, by default, ultimately to allow their deaths to be someone else's problem.

Because of this, we see ongoing and non-stop *begging to bury* in our communities. Relying on the latest crowdfunding platforms like GoFundMe, where strangers are asked to make online contributions to a family's funeral costs, has simply advanced the mechanism for us to gather "emergency funding." However, the fundamental cause is the same: *poor planning for anticipated and unexpected expenses.* I've seen not just poor, but also middle-class African-Americans turn to crowdfunding—in addition to the all-too-common passing of the plate at church, holding car washes and fish fries, and selling customized T-shirts—to raise burial funds. Whenever elders and family leaders forgo their fiscal stewardship, these disappointing patterns continue to repeat themselves, and each new generation is forced to start from scratch.

This frustrating phenomenon can be seen as a form of the chicken-or-egg argument: Is the issue that Black folks don't care about financial security, so they just aren't inclined to purchase large policies? Or is the root of the problem that insurance companies don't push large policies, and since Black folks *don't know what we don't know*, we don't buy substantive policies that can be used to protect *and* build wealth? Either or both can be true. However, the reality is that, thanks to this book, *now you know.* So, what are you prepared to do?

A subset of Information Omitted—even if it's unintentional and based on a lack of understanding—is that financial companies have not created materials specifically designed to help to explain life insurance to African-Americans like they do in translated marketing materials for other cultural markets. The expectation that, since we speak English, the Black community should be up to speed with the general (read: White) market does not take into consideration that, historically, very different financial educations, financial-literacy levels, and a lack of exposure to wealth-building tools have marked our collective experience.

I have also watched some of the so-called "financial experts" on television tell their audiences, especially young African-Americans, that they don't even need to consider buying life insurance (especially "whole life" policies) unless they have dependents or significant disposable income. The detriment here is that such a generalized statement omits an explanation of the positive attributes and power of insurance as a wealth-building tool. This misinformed, blanket recommendation also fails to provide young African-Americans with a comparison as to how others are using insurance to benefit their families in ways that African-Americans are not.

That recommendation also doesn't take into consideration the possible change in health of that individual, and the advantage of the ability to lock in insurability while they are young—especially in a community whose members frequently suffer from diabetes, hypertension, and obesity. These are all factors that will significantly affect one's ability to purchase insurance later in life.

In addition, such a recommendation also fails to address the possible broader use of insurance in the Black community for financial stability and economic growth.

Action Committed

There is also a subtle difference in the marketing, and a purposeful segmentation of the messages and imagery, used by those in the life insurance industry. Think about the commercials for life insurance that we see on television and in print media that show a young White couple being told that they can get protection for their family with $500,000 in coverage for the husband at just $30 a month, and $250,000 in protection for the wife at half that amount. In contrast, in other life insurance advertising, we largely see elderly Black couples discussing final expenses, and having just enough insurance to bury themselves.

Perhaps this is that chicken-or-egg scenario yet again: If insurers believe that Blacks don't buy larger policies to assist with long-term, strategic financial planning, then they only show them small policy amounts adequate enough to cover burial expenses. However, how will African-American investors know to buy larger polices if they are never shown that option? Clearly, the industry's ongoing failure to show us a full range of options does not help to position insurance within the African-American community as a tool for income protection, planning, and financial growth.

I have also noticed another popular opinion of some financial pundits, and the philosophy of several insurance companies, that encourages individuals to buy "term" insurance. That type of insurance is traditionally less expensive, since it only provides coverage for a defined term, as opposed to whole life insurance, which is more expensive but provides coverage for the duration of your lifetime. Some pundits would argue that it is better to take the difference between the higher whole life policy premium and the lower term policy premium and invest that difference in the stock market or other investments.

I find this aforementioned investment recommendation to be a tremendous disservice to the Black community. While it may be a great idea in theory, or a more financially viable option for some members of our community, it is well documented that, fiscally, African-Americans are one of the most conservative racial groups and among the least likely to invest in the stock market. According the *Forbes* article, "The Retirement Crisis Facing African Americans" (March 9, 2017), "Black investors typically focus on guaranteed or fixed investments that are low-risk or no-risk. As a result, their retirement funds aren't compounding at a high rate of return." In other words, we're more apt to invest in fixed income and low-risk or no-risk options (including bonds) as opposed to higher-risk ones (including equities, via the stock market)—or not invest AT ALL!

Therefore, in most cases, the stock-market-investment option advocated by this strategy ultimately doesn't happen in our community. Of equal concern to me is what happens when individuals outlive their term insurance or when the increasing annual premiums make the cost of the term product unmanageable, or their health changes and they become uninsurable when it's time to renew their term insurance. We should also note that factors like credit scores, driving record, and criminal record (specifically, felony convictions) are often considered during the underwriting process for life insurance when deciding the level of risk that an individual poses, beyond the usual factors of health and age. Since many African-Americans are carrying these "red-flags," it may be disproportionately harder for individuals in the Black community to qualify for coverage. Furthermore, because use of these factors is not commonly known, some of us may be disqualified without knowing why, or understanding what we can do to increase our eligibility.

In addition to areas of miseducation, my conversations with African-Americans about their reticence to use insurance and other financial tools has also brought into question actions committed against our communities that have betrayed our "trust"—specifically, actions committed by both companies and individual agents and financial advisors.

When we think about issues of trust specific to life insurance, let's start here: It's absolutely true that African-Americans were overcharged by a large majority of insurance companies when race was still considered a factor in underwriting. According to a *Northwestern Journal of Law & Social Policy* article from fall 2009 titled, "Ending Jim Crow Life Insurance Rates": "From the late 1800s, companies began to charge higher premium rates to cover Black children and reduced benefits of Black adults by one-third to cover their 'excessive' mortality." Another underhanded practice was to advance the age of African-American policyholders by five years or more. Neither of these schemes is taking place now because they are legally prohibited nationwide.

In addition, a questionable number of agents have operated in a self-serving manner—recommending the insurance products that paid the highest commission rather than those that best served their clients. There were also cases in which universal life policies that were strongly recommended by agents ended up crashing—because they were tied to the stock market. Likewise, there were insurance companies that were sold, went out of business, or that flat out neglected to pay their policyholders despite years of dutiful policyholder' payments. For those consumers concerned with whom to trust today, later in this book I will make suggestions as to how you can select appropriate and reputable companies and agents.

THE ENEMY WITHIN: SELF-DEFEATING THINKING IN THE AFRICAN-AMERICAN COMMUNITY

Just as concerning and equally damaging as the external Actions Committed and Information Omitted is the third category: "The Enemy Within." This reflects the ways that some African-Americans have talked themselves out of purchasing—or even being open to hearing about the investment benefits of—life insurance products.

As noted above, the reasons for not acquiring any life insurance or for settling for inadequate life insurance vary. However, some of the self-imposed reasons—often rooted in fear and distrust—include:

- Feeling guilty about profiting off the death of a loved one;
- Justifying not leaving an inheritance for others, courtesy of a "bootstraps" mentality;
- Believing that family members will waste the inheritance;
- Feeling overconfident in the safety net provided by a job or union benefits;
- Assuming that one's family will be taken care of by other relatives or the church;
- Rationalizing that "I just need enough to bury me;" and
- "I'm young, so I don't need to worry about that yet."

So where should we turn and to whom shall we turn if so many of us are lacking knowledge about money management and financial tools like life insurance?

The following chapters will provide details and clarity on what to do to build your personal economic plan—including where to start, how to track your progress, and how to connect with those around you. We will continue to focus on recognizing and overcoming some of the stumbling blocks to creating Black wealth. This instruction will be more than one product, one company, and/or one financial strategy. It's going to be methodical, logical, and all encompassing in your financial life. It will focus on you first, then your family, and next your community.

The exercises at the end of each chapter are intended to help you to take an immediate action step that cumulatively forms an action plan. I will also continue to recommend the tools, tips, and financial strategies to build the wealth that has been withheld from us, or that we ignore, underutilize, or underleverage in our community. We will also continue to add to the discussion of the areas highlighted in the wealth-gap study in order to learn how to come together to close the gap for ourselves and have a greater impact on our community and society.

There's a great quote from the civil rights icon, Rev. Dr. Willie T. Barrow, who worked as an organizer for Dr. Martin Luther King, Jr. during the '60s: "We are not so much divided, as we are disconnected." If you're ready to be part of this movement, then let's get connected.

And let's get to work!

THE UNTOLD RULES FOR BLACK PROSPERITY AND LEGACY

RULE #1. KNOW YOURSELF, KNOW YOUR WORTH

In order to properly discuss wealth-building and legacy-planning strategies for the Black community, we must first learn to value and appreciate the biggest asset that we have in our lives: *ourselves.* This concept of (literally) calculating our personal economic value and worth to ourselves and our families, and then using that number as a foundation for building our path to wealth, has been the first major missing and Untold Rule in financial-planning strategies for the Black community. This chapter will discuss ways that we can calculate the economic value of our lives, in order to reframe our mindset and position us for future financial benefits, while also advancing the cause of collective social and economic impact on our communities.

Before we get to the life-value formulas, we must first note the effects of purposeful conditioning on our community that challenge our mindset and self-worth. To start, many in our community have been made to believe that our personal value is tied to tangible items that can be bought and accumulated (e.g., what brand of car we drive, purse we carry, watch that adorns our wrist, or sneakers we wear). This concept is perpetuated by celebrities, entertainers, and marketers for major companies that promote fashion and image as a benchmark for valuation and validation.

Playing into the instant-gratification mindset of the modern brain, many in our community have adopted this philosophy.

The flaw in this practice of purchasing products instead of making investments is that the basic habit of buying and valuing things that depreciate has only led the majority of our community to consume excessively, and to continually spend to keep up with the latest product models and trends. It also causes us to sacrifice accumulation of foundational assets in exchange for the flash and feel of momentary pleasures.

We enthusiastically relinquish our earnings to the benefit of others before our earnings can at least minimally serve us. This perpetuates an unsustainable cycle of creating the appearance of wealth without creating *actual* wealth. Within this realm of misguidance to obtain luxury products as an external reflection of ourselves, and the worth we desire *others* to place on us, many individuals have become engaged in reckless or extreme behavior to obtain these products by making regrettable financial and personal choices.

A July 2008 study, called "Conspicuous Consumption and Race," supported and published by a network of institutions (including The University of Chicago) revealed that Blacks devote a larger share of their overall expenditures to consumption items that are readily visible to observers as opposed to Whites from similar socioeconomic backgrounds. Automobiles, clothing, and jewelry are examples of these forms of "visible" consumption. Blacks spend about 25 percent more on visible goods than their White counterparts, after accounting for differences in permanent income (meaning ongoing income, as opposed to variable income). The study found these expenditure differences in all sub-groups, except older households. Moreover, researchers found that these racial gaps have been relatively constant over the past seventeen years and that the gaps are economically significant: The absolute annual dollar differential for visible consumption is on the order of $1,900, which is a non-trivial quantity given the average income of African-Americans.

The impact of these choices ranges from the accumulation of excessive credit card debt to criminal behavior. We compound our already difficult financial situations by layering on decisions that have life-altering consequences in pursuit of superficial manifestations of wealth and success.

I have traveled around the world and throughout the country promoting to diverse audiences the concepts of self-worth and self-valuation and that we are worth more than we have been taught to think we are. In doing so, I have witnessed an awakening of consciousness among my audiences as the light bulbs go off about long-hidden self-worth—a worth completely independent of material yardsticks. The quantifying of our current and future economic value and worth to ourselves and our families not only lays a new financial foundation to build upon; it also creates intellectual and emotional enlightenment. Developing a stronger sense of self as a producer, contributor, and builder—rather than a consumer—actually begins to break the deep historic conditioning that is prevalent in our community that we are worth less than others. A stronger sense of self in these areas ultimately leads to a stronger sense of self as protector, leader, and financial steward—building blocks of a strong Black family and a thriving community.

DEVELOPING A STRONGER SENSE OF SELF AS A PRODUCER, CONTRIBUTOR, AND BUILDER—RATHER THAN A CONSUMER

THEY SAID I WAS WORTH $2.5 MILLION!

After two years of working at one of the largest financial service companies in the world, within its Cultural Marketing Department that focused on Hispanic, Black, and several sub-segments of the Asian community, I became curious about getting to the root of the differences in understanding and using of long-term financial investments—like life insurance—among different cultures and ethnicities. As I began to look deeper into this, I was unexpectedly introduced to my own human-life valuation.

It happened when I completed a two-year corporate-leadership-development program and was promoted to an Assistant Vice President role within the company. As recognition and appreciation for this accomplishment, I received a letter from the Human Resources Department congratulating me on my promotion. The letter also stated that, as a newly appointed officer within the company, they wanted my approval for them to place a $2.5 million insurance policy on my life, which would benefit the company's retirement fund upon my death, as they would be the beneficiary. Yes, I was worth...$2.5 million!

The letter went on to explain that the company would pay the premiums, and the policy would stay active even if I left the company. All I had to do was sign on the dotted line. It was such a common practice within the company that it didn't even require a face-to-face conversation or consultation. Their assumption was that I was familiar with this standard practice, which had been so readily accepted by so many before me. Of course, I ultimately signed, but not before following up with several work colleagues to inquire about it. Their explanation stunned me. They told me that it was pro forma across corporate America to insure executives in the company with corporate-owned life insurance (COLI), and that many other companies did so, including banks with bank-owned life insurance (BOLI).

In fact, they detailed how small businesses follow a similar concept by placing "key man" policies on their organization's key leaders to create long-term benefits for their company. The common explanation is that these policies could serve multiple purposes: keeping the business afloat with operating capital, assisting it to buy out partners, and helping leadership to transition if something happened to a key employee. While I understood and accepted this concept of implementing a key man policy for a company's benefit, what was more baffling and thought provoking was to understand where on earth that $2.5 million number for *me*—in particular—came from. Their response was simple: $2.5 million was my "economic value" to the firm.

Needing even further clarification, I asked how the company arrived at that number. I learned that there are several ways to mathematically calculate a person's economic human-life value. The easiest method for someone my age was to create a current-value calculation of my future lifetime earnings. So, for me, the company simply calculated the formula based on my being a 30-year-old junior executive, making $100,000 a year at the time, and the expectation that I would work at least another 25 years until reaching a minimum retirement age of 55. This would provide a conservative value for me of $2.5 million ($100,000 per year X 25 years = $2.5 million). In fact, during those 25 years of future employment I would be sure to earn at least $2.5 million as a base salary before even factoring in bonuses, raises, promotions or any additional deferred contributions to my retirement fund.

Wow! Having never been introduced to, or having had reason to think about, my economic value before, this blew my mind. After a few minutes, I could see that it was a savvy way for them to offset what they were going to pay me for 25 years via an appreciating investment vehicle (key man insurance), which would return that $2.5 million in value back to them upon my death. What became clearer to me was that this life insurance policy was being used as the closest evaluator of *my true replacement value*—like my car insurance would pay for replacing my car with an identical one if I were to get into an accident or my home owner's insurance would pay to me if my house were to burn down. So if anything happened to me, that $2.5 million is what it would cost my employer to "replace me," and the level of work that I did for them.

As eye opening as this revelation was, it paled in comparison to the realization that set in when one of my colleagues asked me incredulously, "Don't you have that much life insurance on yourself?" To which I replied, "NO!" My colleague persisted by asking: "*Why not?*" He went on...

> *Don't you realize that if you get hit by a bus and don't make it home tomorrow, then your wife and children would not receive that $2.5 million of future earnings? Hence, they probably wouldn't be able to live the life to which they have become accustomed. Your children probably won't go on to the colleges you had in mind, and your life's dreams for them would be curtailed. Your church also wouldn't receive your tithing on that income.*

And on he went....

As I sat back and thought about what I'd heard—and reflected upon the long list of possible ways that this lack of adequate coverage would impact my life and that of my family—all I could think about was how much of a departure this ideology was from what I had previously believed and been taught. At that time, I thought I had very little in the way of money and assets. In my mind, all I had in this world was $60,000 in student loan debt, an eleven-year-old Honda Accord with 189,000 miles on it, and a condo on Miami Beach that I purchased with 3% down payment as a first-time home buyer—so even that was all mortgage debt in my mind. In addition, I was contributing just enough to my 401(k) to get my 3% match, and I had a little savings cushion in the bank.

To tell you the truth, I was actually feeling bad about my level of debt and what I thought was a relatively small net worth and tangible-asset value at that point in my life. I had been sacrificing by not buying name brands or keeping up with modern fads like many of my friends. Instead, I'd sacrificed in order to buy a home and to save a little toward retirement. The result was that I certainly didn't see myself as being worth a couple of million dollars to anyone. Particularly as a Black man in America, who was not a rapper or a baller, there was nothing telling me—historically, socially, or experientially—that I was worth *that* much.

This whole new concept and mindset took some time for me to digest, and I thought about the single greatest influence on me regarding the topic of money: my parents. Both were high school graduates who believed in hard work and basic fiscal discipline (buy a home, get a job with a pension and benefits, and so forth). We never had conversations about larger strategic financial planning.

More importantly, like most Black families, the idea of even broaching how much money my parents had and what they did with it was always taboo. Throughout our communities, this pervasive "we don't talk about money" attitude is contributing to our current situation, and its negative impact is exacerbated by the fact that financial education for other cultures starts in childhood. I want to give kudos to rapper and businessman Jay-Z for reversing this trend of not talking to children in the Black community about money while they are young. His recent song, "Legacy," is a verbal will to Jay-Z and Beyoncé's first daughter, Blue Ivy, who was five years old at the time that the song was released.

On the track, Jay-Z is having a deep money conversation with his daughter who is barely out of pre-school (let that sink in). He advises Blue Ivy about how to spend the financial resources that her parents worked so hard to build for the Carter family. He suggests that she consider starting an institute to "put poor kids in school," and states that he would like to see a considerable portion of those resources go to "fund ideas from people who look like we." This conversation is powerful beyond measure. In addition to acknowledging that Blue Ivy is well positioned to be wealthy, Jay-Z is encouraging her to use her inherited resources to help support the less fortunate and to invest in entrepreneurs of color. Although he addresses Blue Ivy directly, this guidance applies equally to his twins, Rumi and Sir, as well. This parental advice is really societal advice for the rest of us: There is tremendous power in learning about finances—early and often.

In light of all the life factors that helped to mold my self-perception, it took me several years to accept the personal valuation attributed to me by my company, and for me to purchase the recommended $2.5 million in life insurance not just for the company's benefit, but a separate policy for my own benefit, and that of my family. Why? Because even though I have an MBA and consider myself savvier than most about finances and economics, I struggled to truly appreciate the idea of my own economic valuation—and the large total that I was given. It also dawned on me that I was not the only one and that this life-value concept was likely equally foreign to many others in the Black community.

As I reflect back on the nearly 20 years since this awakening, I am heartbroken to think about how others valued me more than I valued myself, and that this is the case for many in my community. The awakening associated with understanding your value and your worth also brings about a painful reality—one of sacrifice. I spent the next several years being endlessly conflicted, watching fancy cars go by in my neighborhood while mine (which ran just fine, and was paid off) wasn't as nice. I also felt this way as I watched my favorite programs on an old, 20-inch-tube television while others lined up to get new 40-inch flat screens.

There was a part of me that envied them, even though I knew that most of them probably couldn't afford those purchases. While it was a struggle, it was manageable because I knew that I was doing the right thing through my deferred gratification in order to actually build a sound financial foundation based on real investments and not symbols of wealth. With this awakening, however, witnessing the self-destructive conduct of so many people around me, who were oblivious to the financial reality that I was now keenly aware of, was the real tragedy. My passion to contribute to this movement to close the wealth gap was born out of that realization.

WHAT IS A BLACK LIFE WORTH?

This new paradigm of thought around my personal value—which I had never encountered before, and had only stumbled upon because of a workplace practice—now led me to ask an even greater question: *What is a Black life worth?*

Over time, I came to find out that, for some, the thought of placing a dollar value on ourselves is offensive. Several years ago, while a team of us was conducting a financial-planning seminar for a number of Black attendees, a group of women actually became angry and defensive when we asked: "How much are you worth?" Their collective reply was basically: "You can't put a price tag on me!" It is important to understand that it is common practice in other cultures to make this type of inquiry because they recognize that the next logical action step, born out of this understanding of one's own economic value, is to then work to protect, build, leverage, and pass on the dollar amount of that calculated value to their children so that each generation is no longer starting at zero. This is where building wealth truly starts. It requires that we remove emotion from the valuation exercise, which, particularly in light of our history of enslavement, can be difficult for some members of the Black community.

Although it might be subconscious, I also completely understand the historical sensitivity associated with such a question, which—while neutral on its face—for Black people, in particular, can be highly offensive. For centuries in the U.S.—and other parts of the Western Hemisphere and the world—we were chattel (human property) and literally had a price tag placed on us to serve and build the wealth of *others.* Since that time, valuation of our lives in hard-currency terms has been an unspoken and emotional subject. Even along our hundred-year journey through the Jim Crow era and the Civil Rights Movement, we were still not ready to even *gently* discuss anything resembling an auction-block valuation of a person of African descent. But let's take a moment today, in this new context, to examine the practice of how a slave owner would place an economic value on each individual Black person he owned, just as he would any other chattel and property.

For some slave owners, insuring their "cargo" began during transportation from Africa, when many enslaved Africans lost their lives on ships due to starvation, overcrowding, disease, murder, and even some who preferred to jump overboard rather than to become permanently enslaved. Upon arrival, the valuation would be based on an individual slave's skills, abilities, and earnings potential. The slave master also took into consideration that slave's children in perpetuity, and their expected future earnings as an additional stream of income and profit for himself. In making a specific and detailed calculation, he clearly knew the economic value of a Black life, and even purchased life insurance on those slaves to protect his investment.

To emphasize the significance of this point, regarding value, let's conduct an analysis of the historic life insurance policies that were taken out on the lives of enslaved Africans. In 2002, five hundred such policies were donated to New York City's Schomburg Center for Research in Black Culture by New York Life Insurance Company. Taken from its own sales records, New York Life Insurance Company had provided these to the Schomburg as a source of historical reference material. Those particular policies, issued in the 1840s, showed a face value of $500 purchased on each of the lives of acclimated slaves—"acclimated" meaning their free will had been broken, and they had been trained and trusted to follow instructions.

If we look at an equivalent value of that $500 today, with a 5% growth rate for 170 years, it would be equal to $2 million. Those who knew these calculations and traded these commodities at the time understood how truly valuable, economically, we were as a people and the benefits of taking out insurance policies on us as an investment. We now need to see that same value *in* ourselves, and *for* ourselves, by using this same value concept—but with a new level of detachment and objectivity.

Doing this valuation, based on my own current earnings potential, helped me to realize that I am a living, breathing *million-dollar asset*. By failing to conduct such valuations today, we are missing out on the big picture that encompasses the totality of who we are. Such a valuation isn't solely based on paychecks or tax returns but on the economic magnitude of who we *are,* beyond accumulated symbols of wealth.

Once we truly understand that, at a psychic and cellular level, it becomes unconscionable for us to continue to spend millions of dollars (present and future) without purpose, priority, and proper placement of that money so that it can increase exponentially. That potential misplacement of financial priorities applies to all of us. Thus, we have to undertake a concerted effort to promote and instill this concept of considering and quantifying our earnings potential in order to enable us to make more prudent financial decisions; act differently; have higher expectations of ourselves, our families, and communities; and to orchestrate more profitable and financially sound outcomes.

I have noticed that there is one common instance in which we galvanize, as a community, around a million-dollar self-valuation, and that is when there is a calamity or catastrophe. When someone gets killed in an accident, as a wrongful death, or under unjust circumstances, the family of that individual will often look to sue the insurance company or the governmental institution involved for millions of dollars. Now that we have broadened our view regarding this topic, let's not reserve these million-dollar calculations for these unfortunate circumstances. Let's employ these higher valuations every day, across our entire lives, and in every realm—education, employment, social justice, political activism, and economic stability.

TAKING CARE OF YOUR MILLION-DOLLAR ASSET

It wasn't long before it dawned on me that if I had an asset worth one million dollars—a house, car, or a prize-winning racehorse, for instance—I would go to great lengths to take care of it. In fact, if a horse could earn me one million dollars I would most certainly not have it eating fried food covered in salt; drinking alcohol and using drugs; or hanging out into the wee hours of the morning. Instead, I'd make sure that it was getting proper exercise and adequate amounts of sleep, and I would *definitely* make sure that it visited the veterinarian on a regular basis for preventative care. Let's go deeper into this point. In thinking about this horse as my moneymaker, I would not want to put it into hazardous situations, and I would *most definitely* want to partner it with another horse of similar value to mate and to plan a future for them and their offspring. Through this pairing, the value of that offspring would also increase.

Once I acknowledged how I would take care of my hypothetical million-dollar horse, it became unbelievable for me to think that I wasn't taking care of myself in the same way—particularly once I knew that I was worth $2.5 million! Likewise, many of us in the Black community are not taking care of our health, are engaging in reckless behavior, and are making poor life decisions. In addition—and I know I'll be stepping on some toes here—some of us have a more selective vetting process for choosing our cars than we do for choosing our mates (Ouch!). When dating, the pleasure principle is not enough. Your ultimate intention should be to find a like-minded and compatible life partner so both of you can build an empire and a legacy together. Yes, marriage is a union of two minds, spirits, and hearts, but it's also an *economic* union and a financial contract. We must guard and manage *every* aspect of our lives, on the same level as we would our million-dollar assets.

The bright side of my finally realizing and accepting that I was a $2.5 million asset was the subsequent transformation of both my mindset and expectations in life. When I truly embraced that evolved mentality, I felt empowered, both psychologically and financially. Now, like an athlete getting a five-year contract for several million dollars per year or someone receiving stock options in a startup company (who gets the ownership, but not the cash and value upfront), I can see the value in long-term planning as my millions in earnings roll in over the next 20 to 30 years. I realized that I didn't have to live solely in the moment, under the misguided assumption that my future might not be any brighter than my present.

I realized that I *can* make smarter decisions and have higher expectations for my future. I *can* visualize and ask myself how much I will save for retirement, insure myself against injury, and give back to the people and organizations that I love. I can also think about the mark that I want to leave on this world. That one realization enabled me to engage in long-term, strategic planning, both personally and professionally, without fear.

I realized that imparting these financial lessons to my children would prepare them for early success. I also acknowledged my responsibility to teach them early on, so that they wouldn't fall victim to the trappings of reality TV and modern music, which glorify the "YOLO" (You Only Live Once) attitude of destructive consumerism. While such extravagance is often celebrated by celebrities on TV and in music, the subsequent, long-term impact of unaccumulated and unmanifested wealth is rarely highlighted, nor the regret for not making better choices. I want to make sure that my children will be able to create and give even more to the world than I did.

OUR MODERN-DAY RALLY CRY

It's amazing to think that it was nearly 50 years ago that Rev. Jesse Jackson, Sr. rallied the Black community in the Civil Rights Movement around the poem and chant, "I Am—*Somebody*!" The intent was to demand that mainstream America recognize and appreciate African-Americans as equal to everyone else with regard to human and constitutional rights. It was also used to motivate Black students. As successful as that chant was, we have witnessed another modern-day rallying cry rise up over the past few years, exclaiming, "Black Lives Matter!" Like its predecessors in the 1960s and 1970s, it's a call for equal treatment and respect from society.

It signifies a campaign against violence and systemic racism. And it's a rallying cry to our nation to value Black brilliance and our positive contributions to America. With the "Black Lives Matter!" slogan firmly embedded in this country's psyche and discourse, I believe that we can use it as a springboard to open up an expanded dialogue about what a Black life is worth: "Black Lives *and Black Wealth* Matter!" Similarly, we should now say, *"I Am—Somebody: A million-dollar asset to my community and the world!"* This can be the next step in the progression of us as a people—evolving from having a civil rights, social justice, and politically centric focus, to becoming economically savvy and strong.

I AM—SOMEBODY: A MILLION-DOLLAR ASSET TO MY COMMUNITY AND THE WORLD!

I am concerned that the constant barrage of media images highlighting stories of African-American men getting shot and going to jail has desensitized so many of us in this country and caused us to devalue and discount the lives and potential contributions of Black men—particularly younger men. More disturbing is that these young men devalue each other and themselves to such a degree that they are cavalier about taking each other's lives or engaging in overtly reckless conduct, causing them to risk forfeiting their own futures for death or incarceration. In cities like Chicago and Baltimore, we've seen such murders in action for far too long. As a result, I've sometimes heard it said that "Black lives *don't* matter to other Black people either."

This new focus on personal value serves as a profound catalyst in this overall dynamic of us devaluing our own lives, as Black people. It can lay the groundwork for heightened self-respect and respect for each other on all fronts. We've been anesthetized over decades to such killings, conditioned to neither see nor understand the impact of both the losses of these lives and of the economic value associated with both those who have been murdered and those who are incarcerated for committing the murders. However, with the paradigm shift that valuation brings, the associated dollar loss to that individual's family and our community becomes readily clear, and—as it naturally should—a lost life now has deeper meaning for everyone.

To see it this way sheds a new light on some of the forces keeping us from getting ahead financially. Consider the crime statistics provided by the FBI: In 2016, the number of Black homicide victims nationally totaled 7,881. This one-year statistic easily confirms that at least 10,000 Black men have been shot since Trayvon Martin was killed in 2012. As each one of those men will no longer earn one million dollars over the next 20 to 40 years their deaths and/or incarceration will have taken a collective $10 billion away from our families and communities (10,000 men X $1,000,000 of earnings over 20 years = $10 billion). In fact, that 10,000 figure is an *underestimation*—and just a drop in the bucket.

Even more alarming was an April 20, 2015 article in *The New York Times*, titled, "1.5 million Black Men Missing" that opens as follows:

> *In New York, almost 120,000 black men between the ages of 25 and 54 are missing from everyday life. In Chicago, 45,000 are, and more than 30,000 are missing in Philadelphia. Across the South—from North Charleston, S.C., through Georgia, Alabama and Mississippi and up into Ferguson, Mo.—hundreds of thousands more are missing. They are missing, largely because of early deaths or because they are behind bars....*

In the same vein as the previous tabulation, but taking it up a notch, we can use this calculation for a human-life valuation of the over one million Black men currently in prison, jail, or tied to the parole system. At a potential of $1,000,000 each in lost future earnings over the next 20 years, 1,000,000 men x $1,000,000 in earnings equates to a $1 trillion deficit in wages, contributions, and community and national impact. We already see the ripple effects of this deficit playing out daily in ongoing poverty, hopelessness, and violence. We must ultimately work to stop this mass financial hemorrhage being created in our community, day after day, year after year, generation after generation.

OUR VALUE BEYOND WHAT WE EARN

As we continue to delve more deeply into this discussion, I want to point out that there is still more to your value in life beyond what you earn and can produce. This is especially important to note in case you are currently unemployed, underemployed, in the wrong job, or are further along in life with fewer years of earnings potential. I want you to know that you still have value—above and beyond the human-life-value calculation.

This additional value that I'm referring to is unique to human beings in that we have life experiences, varying skills, marketability, potential, purpose, passion, and plans that we intend to execute. We have possibilities, hopes, dreams, and aspirations that we want to fulfill. We also have people who love and need us who, statistics say, are destined for poverty, jail, victimization, and/or violence (or all four). These are the people who we need to teach, touch, and protect; this is what makes us even more valuable than our life-value calculation alone! We must be persistent in finding ways to unearth those treasures by achieving the desires embedded deep in our hearts.

Part of our value is our aspiration to create a legacy based on those things that we want to be known and remembered for—through the difference that we make in the world, in our community, and in the lives of our children and grandchildren. Such things enhance and increase our worth!

In addition to the life-value calculation we outlined for wealth building and planning purposes, we are still worth even more, based on things that are incalculable. It is from this position that I present this book. When I think about the value taken from us during slavery that has never truly been returned; when I think about the graveyard being the richest place on earth because of all of the great ideas, inventions, intentions, and desires that were never executed and fulfilled; and when I think about the greatness of our race, the perseverance of our spirit, and the contributions that we have made to this world, I want us to harness all that we have, and all that we are, to achieve all that we can.

As I sit and write this book in 2018, thinking about the political and social-justice storms currently brewing over our communities, I wish to see the same fervor rallied around the idea that not only do Black Lives Matter, but *Black Wealth Matters.* This is because an increase in our economic aptitude and collective net worth are things within our control, that have the power to change the landscape for Black people in America so that we will no longer even have to assert that Black Lives Matter. Yes, we still need to be politically active, but our collective wealth, and the power that comes from it will be our *loudest* megaphone!

I want us to be intentional about creating a strong and positive outlook for ourselves, based on our value and our worth. I want us to better appreciate each other, and to work together to change our community with a mindset geared toward collective growth and progress. I am going to conclude this chapter by reminding you: *Know Yourself, Know Your Worth*!

Now that you know what you likely didn't know before about this life-altering practice of economic valuation, my question to you: What are YOU going to do with this information?

IF WE EVER COME TOGETHER: MILLION-DOLLAR-ME ACTION STEP

Please take a minute to calculate your economic value and worth as a new starting point to building your path to wealth. Then pause and think about how you feel after seeing the calculation confirm that you are a million-dollar asset—and potentially worth far more than you ever dreamed!

Life-value wealth calculation:

Current Salary × *Number of years left to work until retirement* = *present value of future earnings*

Diagram 5. For your reference, here is a simple chart based on retiring at age 67, with varying salaries across the top, and current age on the left-hand side:

Diagram 5.

Present Age	*$35,000*	*$50,000*	*$75,000*	*$100,000*
25	1,470,000	2,100,000	3,150,000	4,200,000
30	1,295,000	1,850,000	2,775,000	3,700,000
35	1,120,000	1,600,000	2,400,000	3,200,000
40	945,000	1,350,000	2,025,000	2,700,000
45	770,000	1,100,000	1,650,000	2,200,000
50	595,000	850,000	1,275,000	1,700,000
55	420,000	600,000	900,000	1,200,000
60	245,000	350,000	525,000	700,000

RULE #2.
INSURE YOURSELF—
TO ENSURE YOUR FUTURE

When I first met the late Cirilo McSween, who in 1957 became the first Black agent to cross the color barrier and join a large, White life insurance company, I asked him why he felt he needed to be a financial services pioneer. He said that he was tired of seeing our community not getting ahead economically. He decided that he would present and sell life insurance differently than the traditional debit agents who had been selling only burial policies to our communities around the country up until that point. He determined that the greatest change in financial planning that he could make for our community was to help its members create *estates* for themselves, and to see the value of leaving behind *legacies* for those they loved.

In reflecting on that conversation, I've realized that Mr. McSween was far ahead of his time with this message and approach. He was progressive and forward thinking when the words *estate* and *legacy* were still uncommon terms in our community. Disturbingly, 60 years later, this is still largely the case. These financial concepts tend to be reserved for other communities—and high-net-worth clients in particular. We should expand our understanding and actions to now incorporate *estate* into our vocabulary and match what others have been doing and building for generations.

The concepts of creating a financial safety net and establishing an estate represent another opportunity to reverse the negative conditioning that started in slavery—and has continued ever since—whereby we perceive ourselves as not having anything of value. This further leads us to believe that we shouldn't even bother attempting to create financial value in our communities, because we are so far away from the goals of self-sustainability and financial freedom that it seems out of our grasp. On the contrary, if we can wrap our arms around the idea of developing safety nets and building estates, we can stop living from day-to-day, merely existing and getting by, or justifying the squandering of our existing resources in *the moment*, because YOLO: *You Only Live Once.*

In this chapter, I will present my findings from having analyzed, since 2001, the specific differences in perception and utilization of life insurance as a financial tool for both the creation of family safety nets and estates within the Black community. In doing so, we can demystify and better leverage insurance.

Next, I will illustrate how others have been using insurance to create generational wealth and legacies in a manner that we've been unaware of. I'm also going to present a new way to view your own wealth and personal estate once you've added this investment instrument to your financial portfolio.

I will conclude with thoughts on the kinds of insurance you should consider and the entities from whom—ideally—you should purchase that insurance from, so that you can join our wealth movement to change the financial future of Black America. This section is dedicated to the memory and mission of Mr. McSween who told me that he was passing me the proverbial baton, in order to ensure that the work he so loved—financially empowering the Black community and using life insurance as a foundational building block—would continue.

GETTING INSURED: THINK *BUILD*—NOT *BILLS*

Now that I have provided you with both an understanding of and proof that *you* are indeed your own greatest asset (not just a million-dollar, but a multi-million-dollar asset in most cases), as discussed in the last chapter, your next course of action should be to insure yourself as you would any other highly valuable asset. This is so that you can guarantee the income stream of your future earnings (human capital), provide protection for your assets (financial capital), and help to fulfill your hopes, dreams, and aspirations in life. The ultimate goal: to ensure your own strong future, as well as that of your family.

Protecting income is one of a family's most important needs—*especially* families that have few assets because their options are limited, and so much is at stake if anything happened to the family's breadwinners. Due to this dynamic, many families remain conservative in their approach to investments and their overall attitude when it comes to seizing opportunities. A given family's key earners can't realistically afford to lose a job, get sick, get divorced, or pass away, as the family would be devastated. Many fear a setback that they can't or won't recover from. This is a tremendous fear within our community in particular, which those with some measure of wealth accumulation might not feel as acutely—and, therefore, might not even think about.

On its most basic level, if you have dependents, like children or a spouse, who would suffer financially if you were to die, life insurance is a necessity—it's the financial safety net that you must create for them. Again, we're looking at the tool of life insurance well beyond the conversation of paying for funeral expenses. Ask yourself: *What would my family do to pay the mortgage or buy groceries if I passed?*

Recognize that life insurance is not only for the breadwinner of a family but also for those other individuals who work and contribute to the household. Even if your family includes a stay-at-home parent, consider what it might cost to replace the work that he or she does for the household. If your spouse were to pass away, would you need to secure day care for your children? Would you need to secure household help? Could you afford these expenses based on your current income?

Life insurance is a tool that covers all of this. It should be considered as a foundational financial building block that you control. Most of us have no plan or are not thinking about a plan, in areas where we should all at least plan for the worst and hope for best. If I had a machine in my garage printing $100 bills, I would certainly insure it. Yes, I recognize my humanity, but, when it comes to taking care of my family, I am akin to that machine.

We talked about our value being tied to future earnings, so you have to protect your income in order to shore up your family's security and strategically contribute to its success. With this in mind, as we examined in the previous chapter, we can calculate your replacement value by a multiple of your income, in the same way you would consider full financial replacement value from insurance if you got into a car accident or if there were damage to your home.

Diagram 6.

Age	*Multiples of Earned Income*
20–30	23–27 ×
31–40	20–23 ×
41–45	16–19 ×
46–50	13–16 ×
51–55	10–12 ×
56–60	8–10 ×
61–65	6–8 ×
66+	5 ×

Diagram 6 is a chart used by many of the major insurance companies. In order to use it to derive the replacement value of a 36-year-old man with an annual income of $65,000, you would calculate his salary by the corresponding multiples for his age (20–23) to arrive at $1.3 million–$1.5 million in life insurance coverage. You not only need to be aware of this valuation for yourself, but, when you purchase insurance, urge the company from which you're purchasing your policy to insure you for the *full* amount at which you're valued

To cover the large insurance policy amounts, term insurance is often the most cost-efficient form of coverage. But you need to think beyond this one product: Consider whole life insurance—alone or in conjunction with term insurance—and also make sure that the term policy (e.g., 5 years, 10 years, 20 years, etc.) doesn't expire while your need for a financial safety net still exists.

As I explained previously: *Term insurance provides coverage at a fixed rate of payments for a limited period of time, and whole life insurance is guaranteed to remain in force for the insured's entire lifetime, provided that he or she pays the required premiums.* I must stress that you should not think of monthly insurance premiums as another bill, but as an investment in the peace of mind that comes from having a safety net. It's a confidence policy that ensures that your family will be provided for after your death. Remember: You are *a million-dollar asset*!

In our community, another important Untold Rule tied to the safety-net concept is for us as African-Americans to lock in our insurability while we are young and healthy. If obesity, diabetes, and/or hypertension are prevalent in your family, then you must purchase insurance while you are young. If you don't, then you risk not being approved for insurance at all later in life or paying vastly higher premiums due to health conditions that insurance companies won't view as favorable. There are many in our community who wish that they had purchased insurance in their 20s and 30s, so I implore you to take this recommendation very seriously. There are only two things you cannot get when you really need them: a parachute and life insurance.

If you are older and/or your health is not the greatest, do not give up hope, as you may be able to obtain a "guaranteed" final-expense policy from one of the many major insurance companies. These policy amounts are typically between $2,000 and $20,000. You can go to the website for the AARP (American Association of Retired Persons; www.aarp.org) to find recommendations and additional information. As the title seems to convey, a final-expense policy can help to cover your burial and—depending on the face amount—could allow you to have enough left over to leave behind a small legacy that can serve as a seed for your loved ones.

Lastly, in addition to insurance, as part of your safety net you should also have emergency savings on reserve. Aim to maintain enough to cover 3 to 6 months of expenses. If you own a home, then build up enough equity to tap into a home-equity loan (but only for *real* emergencies—not things like paying off credit card debt!). A retirement account, such as a 401(k), can also serve as another resource for cash reserves through loans and taxable withdrawals. (Also exercise wisdom and caution when tapping into it!) Your final go-to for liquidity in an emergency should be credit cards, since their interest rates tend to be far higher than the other options I mentioned. I have pulled from each of these sources over time, as needed. If a life event or emergency requires that you draw down from one of these resources, just be sure to pay it back and only leverage it for emergencies and necessities, not wants or desires.

CREATING YOUR ESTATE

There's something very significant about owning an insurance policy, as it relates to our community, in particular, because it is a document that actualizes our worth (to the tune of millions of dollars if that is the size of the policy owned) that we can refer back to over and over again. In essence, possession of such a policy becomes a financial North Star—helping each of our households to stay focused and on course with our wealth-building goals. It also creates the bedrock of an estate.

The financial website, Investopedia, defines an estate as: "All of the valuable things an individual owns, such as real estate, art collections, collectibles, antiques, jewelry, investments and life insurance."

That's right—they said "life insurance." Yet, when members of our community are taught about wealth creation, there continues to be virtually no reference to insurance as a powerful baseline portfolio tool. When you combine a policy with your other financial investments, the final tally may demonstrate a significantly higher financial worth than you might have initially imagined. Let's do a calculation for a fictional estate belonging to a couple in their late 40s to see what goes into an "estate," as covered in the aforementioned definition:

- Family Home ($310k); 401(k)'s ($160k); Checking, Savings, and Investments ($40k):

  Value: $510,000

- Cars, Collectibles, Jewelry (Symbols of Wealth):

  Value: $35,000 (Note that, in the African-American community, a large emphasis is typically placed here. *It's time to change that.*)

- Two Life insurance Policies—tied to personal worth ($1.5 and $1 million):

  Value: $2.5 million

  Total estate valued at over $3 million.

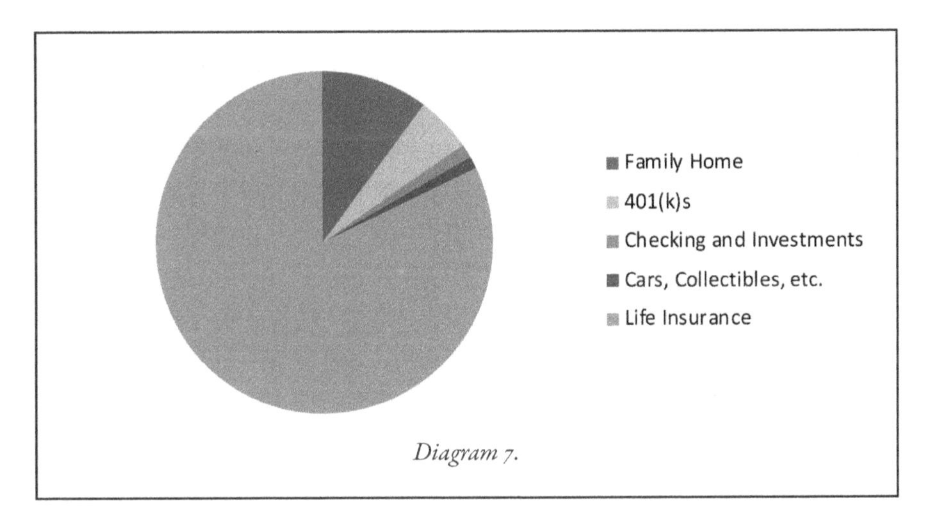

Diagram 7.

The insurance allows this couple to bring their future earnings into their current life assessment and planning. It gives a current picture of their complete value, even though it will be fully realized over time. Like that professional athlete with a million-dollar, five-year contract that doesn't provide all the money upfront, or someone receiving stock options in a company that will mature to full value over a certain number of years, they can begin to look at their personal financial house and think about how they want to grow their estate. They can also think about what future financial fruits they want their estate to bear. This is what I meant about creating a financial North Star, because it allows them to establish a long-term financial destination that they can build their financial path toward, while measuring and tracking its progress.

In addition, the policy allows them to question whether they are conducting themselves according to this valuation—not to show off, but to make the best decisions to actualize and maximize their situation. They can challenge themselves to be accountable by asking: *Am I operating my life and my thinking in a way that reflects that I'm in command of a $3 million estate?* On those days when they are feeling average, overwhelmed, or challenged to just keep up or catch up, they can refer back to their overall estate value and be reminded that they are worth *so* much more. Taking this action also has a positive impact on this couple's mindset. This couple should feel proud and accomplished to be millionaires—even if just on paper!

Next, the owners of this fictional estate would need to speak with their accountant and attorney to discuss creating their wills and trust. They also need to converse with their insurance agent to properly designate beneficiaries. (The chapter that covers Principle #6 will provide further details on some of these advanced-planning topics, including how to establish your power of attorney and medical directives.) Many people believe that if they have a will, their estate planning is complete, but there is much more to a solid estate plan. A good plan is designed to: avoid having your will dragged into probate court for a final determination; save on estate taxes; protect assets if ever you need to move into a nursing home; and appoint someone to act as a trusted advocate for you if you become disabled.

On another note, some of you might have heard over the years that if you don't have financial dependents, then life insurance is not necessary and shouldn't be a piece of your financial safety net. I strongly disagree because I've seen examples of many people who use life insurance as part of their estate-planning and cash-accumulation plans, *regardless* of their dependent status. In fact, they have personally benefitted from the cash accumulation guarantees and tax advantages that many of the whole-life policies offer while they are *alive.* They also use the insurance to pay an inheritance to their family members (e.g., nieces, nephews, cousins) upon *their* own death, as well as to provide gifts to beloved organizations and institutions.

HIDDEN IN PLAIN SIGHT: HOW OTHER COMMUNITIES CAPITALIZE ON INSURANCE

Based on my work at one of the largest life insurance companies in the industry, I have paid particular attention to how other cultures place sizeable life insurance policies on themselves—not only to create sound financial foundations and estates, but, shrewdly, also to obtain investment guarantees and tax-advantaged benefits. They also find ways to efficiently access their policies' cash reserves for themselves over their lifetime—doing so with low interest rates and little paperwork, while making certain that they leave significant financial windfalls. Positioning life insurance this way makes it a powerful foundational asset at the base of a comprehensive financial plan. Thus, it's viewed as an investment, taking insurance beyond the protective role it's traditionally played.

I want to reiterate: *Insurance creates benefits for you while you are alive and guarantees an inheritance for your family.* Here are some of the specific investment benefits that permanent insurance—most specifically, whole life—offers, from which other communities have been benefiting for generations:

INSURANCE CREATES BENEFITS FOR YOU WHILE YOU ARE ALIVE AND GUARANTEES AN INHERITANCE FOR YOUR FAMILY.

- **Life Insurance Dividends**

First and foremost, mutual life insurance companies (not stock companies) serve the needs of current and future policyholders by returning excess operating and investment profits directly to them in the form of dividends, rather than giving those gains to their stock holders (who, incidentally, may or may not also be insurance policyholders of that company as well). Dividends can be: taken as cash payments; used to reduce your premium payment; left on deposit to earn interest; and used to buy more protection, which will increase your death benefit and cash value even more. This practice has gone on for generations and has continued even in times of low national interest rates. (Please note that dividends are not guaranteed.)

- **Investment Guarantees and Tax Advantages**

  a. Whole life insurance provides a guaranteed death benefit so that beneficiaries will not receive less than the amount of the policy;

  b. Whole life premiums are guaranteed never to increase, regardless of your health, the economy, or your age;

  c. The cash value within your whole life policy is guaranteed to grow;

  d. The death benefit income from whole life is tax free to your beneficiaries;

  e. The cash value from your whole life policy will grow tax deferred, meaning that you will not pay income taxes on it, allowing it to grow even faster;

  f. The cash value from your whole life policy is yours to use during your lifetime, and you can usually access it income tax–free.

- **Semi-Compulsory Savings**

Part of your whole life premium payment is applied to the cost of the insurance, and another portion is held in savings. This accumulation, called the cash value, is a reserve for later investment and use. It can be very beneficial to those who find it hard to put money aside for savings on their own.

- **Create Your Own "Bank"**

  The owner of a dividend-paying whole life insurance policy can access his or her cash value as a flexible source of funds without the questions, credit check, or paperwork required for bank loans. The loans will not show up on your credit report or affect your credit score. They will accrue a competitive interest rate, and the money is typically available in a few days. And the loans can be used in any way—as a down payment on a home, to finance a new car, to start a business, or to supplement retirement income. With the repayment of each policy loan, the cash value and death benefit will be fully restored, allowing the owner to access cash value for future events as needed.

- **The Disability Waiver of Premium**

  This life insurance policy feature enables the owner to stop paying policy premiums in the event that he or she becomes disabled, while continuing to receive life insurance coverage.

- **Protection from Creditors**

  A life insurance policy's face amount and cash value are protected from creditors in most states.

- **Exclusion from Financial Aid Forms**

  A life insurance policy's face amount and accumulated cash value are not reported on the Free Application for Federal Student Aid (FAFSA) or included in the consideration for financial aid eligibility.

- **Charitable Giving**

  Life insurance can be used as a substantial, cost-effective gift to charity, while allowing the donor's family to retain other assets. An outright gift of a policy to a charity will create a current

> income-tax charitable deduction equal to the policy's market value. Moreover, a policy donated but still being paid for by the donor will make the premium payments deductible. Lastly, a life insurance gift is private and does not become a matter of public record.

As noted above, many communities have taken advantage of these benefits for hundreds of years and over many generations, to the point that it has become second nature and the greatest, easiest, and surest way of passing down generational wealth. Across the insurance industry, life insurance is used as an *income-producing tool* in this manner. (Yes, I had to highlight that!) The companies collectively payout tens of billions of dollars every year in death claims, of which only a fraction of this wealth transfer goes to African-Americans.

According to the Institute on Assets and Social Policy study, "The Roots of the Widening Racial Gap" (February 2013), Whites are five times more likely to inherit money than African-Americans; and, among those receiving an inheritance, Whites received about ten times more wealth than African Americans. As I've been saying for a long time, this disparity is a key contributor to the racial wealth gap, and finally there are recent articles confirming that inheritance plays a greater part in disproportionally generating wealth than previously thought. A February 2017 article on Bloomberg.com also confirmed this point, starting with its title and subtitle: "The Big Reason Whites Are Richer Than Blacks in America—Inheritance matters a lot more than previously thought. Guess who's getting the lion's share." It doesn't get *more* direct than that!

Finally, I want to say it again: *Those with money will typically safeguard against possible hardship or adversity with different types of insurance, including life insurance.* Hence, they can more confidently make decisions for, and take action on, various life scenarios—whether they live long, healthy lives, become disabled, or die. As a result, they are able to move more boldly in life decisions, such as starting a business, joining the Peace Corps, taking a sabbatical from work, or investing in a new stock recommendation-because they can take greater chances knowing there is a safety net, or a reserve to pull from, for themselves and their families.

WHO SHOULD YOU BUY INSURANCE FROM—AND HOW?

Now you have heard the broad range of reasons why you need to buy life insurance and have learned how others are using theirs. Let's turn our attention to where you are *personally*. For most people, different times in their lives may require more insurance coverage than others. Diagram 8 shows how a person's life insurance needs can change over time:

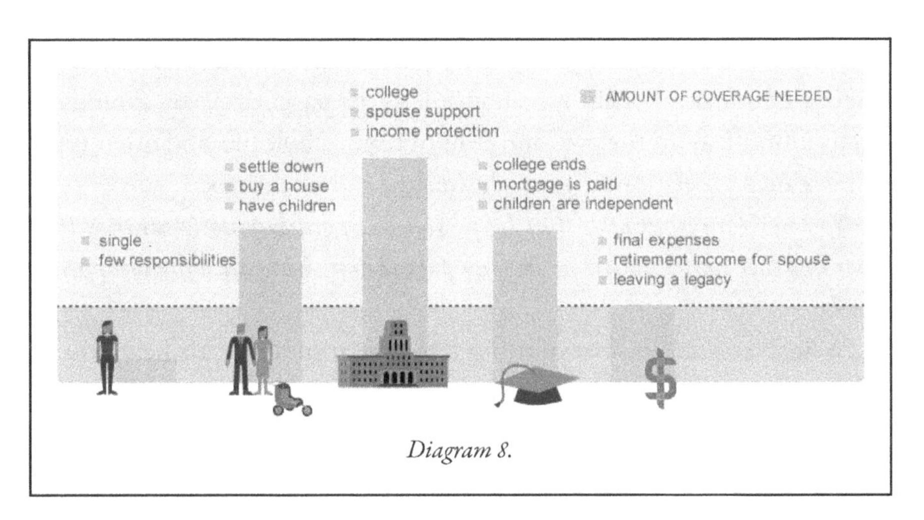

Diagram 8.

On the extreme left, we see an image of a single female who has few responsibilities that would necessitate life insurance, so her amount of coverage needed, as represented by the bar, is low. However, remember that she should still get started on acquiring insurance while she is young and healthy. As her life changes, and we move to the right, we see her get married and settle down, purchase a home, and have children. These life changes cause her coverage needs to rise. (The same holds true for single mothers who should absolutely have insurance in place in case anything were to happen to them.) This need peaks as we continue on to the right: She now needs life insurance to protect her income, help support her spouse, and pay for the college education expenses of her children if something were to happen to her.

Moving on, her coverage needs start to decline as her children finish college, become independent, and she pays off her mortgage. Finally, at the extreme right, her coverage need drops to a lower level. At this stage, her needs are to: be able to provide funds for her retirement income; cover final burial expenses; and to leave a financial legacy for her beneficiaries.

As you can see from this illustration, proper insurance planning requires purposeful thought and active engagement to adequately protect your family and to leverage a policy's many features. Set aside time to do this. Even if you have a term life insurance policy provided by your employer (which usually only matches your annual salary by 1X and is offered as a company benefit for a few dollars per paycheck), you should educate yourself about the pros and cons of term, whole life, and other types of insurance in relation to your age, health, and intentions.

You need an approach that helps you to avoid buying insurance that does not last long enough or buying permanent insurance for temporary needs!

Wherever you are in exploring how life insurance can help you to achieve your short- and long-term financial goals, here are several strategies that can help you to address your evolving needs and fit within your current budget:

1. Buy an initial policy now, perhaps term, and then a supplemental policy later.
2. Lock in your insurability. When determining what to buy when, it's worth remembering that, the younger you are when you buy, the more cost effective it will likely be.
3. Buy a term policy now that covers more than your current needs, as it can help to protect your future.
4. Start with term and convert to permanent policies, like whole life and universal, later.

5. Purchase both term and permanent policies to get the benefits from the different features that they offer.
6. Add optional features, also known as riders, to broaden the coverage that a particular policy provides. For example, adding the disability waiver of premium, that was explained earlier, will continue to pay the policy in the event that you become disabled and are unable to work.

At this point, some of you may want to talk to an adviser about how much insurance is enough. So, with that in mind, and when it's time to buy, I want to provide you with a few additional points to consider regarding companies, agents, and sales concepts. I totally understand that it can be scary to wonder: *To whom should I go when I don't know?* Here is some guidance:

- Research the **reputation and financial strength** of the life insurance companies you're considering. You can look up their rankings and ratings online (visit https://www.insure.com/best-life-insurance-companies/) and check with the Better Business Bureau for any complaints against them. Most companies offer competitive pricing on similar products, but the financial strength and longevity is what you are looking for to make sure that they will be around when you need them, throughout your long life. For this reason, a larger and more solid company might justify slightly higher pricing for their policies. Customer service and a history of paying claims on a timely basis is also important, as you are picking a company to help ease the financial burden on your loved ones who are designated as your beneficiaries in the event of your death. Lastly, consider the conversion-option privileges on the term policies. Since the majority of policies sold are term, having a conversion feature is important because it allows you to change your policy without having to take another medical exam or re-qualify. Remember: *Your term policy is going to expire, and if your health should decline before it does, then you may* *not be insurable after that time.* Not all companies' term insurance policies can be converted.

- Seek those companies that are **committed to you and your community**, and to building and supporting diverse communities and markets overall. I'm not only talking about companies that place ads in community-related media, but also ones that actually have a presence with field offices, employ a racially and culturally diverse workforce—including agents, provide foundation grants and sponsorships, and create opportunities for supplier diversity.
- Assess the **skill set and credentials of the agent** that you are considering for your life insurance needs. Think of your conversation as a type of job interview. Ask if he or she possesses designations and licenses and belongs to any industry organizations. Agents who have continuing-education credentials demonstrate a level of commitment to their careers and a desire to stay informed about industry trends and changes. Inquire whether the agent is an independent one, who represents several life insurance companies, or an agent who works as an employee of one company. The former will provide you with different and competitive quotes from an array of companies, whereas the other will not. Query the agent's years of experience, area of specialty, and success track record. Pay attention to whether that agent follows a process tailored to your particular needs and is not simply providing quick, generic recommendations—clearly your preference is for the former. Ask if life insurance is that agent's primary business. Also find out how you would reach your agent in an emergency and whether there's backup coverage when that agent is away. You are looking for a true insurance and financial services professional, trained to provide the best service and products for you and your family.

Be mindful of opportunities to **seek out and support our many qualified African-American agents,** as there are many out there who are leaders in the industry and at the top of their game. I know that purposely seeking out a Black agent might not always be at the forefront of your mind, but I want to note that other communities do seek out their own agents first. By doing so, they help more of their agents become successful by being their clients. By cycling their dollars, they also make the financial and social fabric of their communities stronger. As conscious consumers and responsible purchasers, let's do the same. The one caveat I have here is that you thoroughly vet the African-American agents using all of the factors listed above, such as their skill set, credentials, affiliations, reputation, and the reliability of the companies for whom they work, as you would for any other agents.

- **Don't be solely led by a company's 'product slogans,' or focus and philosophy.** Examples of a focus or philosophy are: "Buy term and invest the difference," or the opposite, "You only need whole life insurance." Make sure that you are focused on the *purpose and intention of your coverage,* both for the short and long term, as discussed earlier in this chapter. Once you get an estimate on the amount of coverage you'll be receiving, stay within the dollar range you've already allocated in your budget for insurance in order to accomplish your goals.
- **Put your insurance need first, budget second, and product selection third.** Be mindful of insurance companies and agents that lead with product recommendations first, as they may be potentially driven by the commissions that they collect on those sales. Make sure to first assess your insurance needs, then figure out your available budget, and finally select the best-suited product for your circumstances. Make sure you put *you* first!

WRITE THE VISION—MAKE IT PLAIN

Insuring yourself creates an estate with the stroke of a pen and provides many financial benefits that are not maximized in the Black community. I'm sure there are many prominent and affluent families, like the Bushes and Bidens, who know that insurance is the foundation of every sound financial plan—so, like Cirilo McSween, my team and I have been spreading this message to the Brown, Banks, and Barnes families of Harlem, Detroit, New Orleans, and Compton, to let them know as well.

In his classic book, *The 7 Habits of Highly Effective People,* Stephen R. Covey implores us to: "Begin with the end in mind." Ask yourself: At the end of your life, what do you want to have accomplished, and what do you want to be *your* legacy? Then start from where you are *now* and map out a step-by-step plan to get there. The next chapter will provide you with a framework to accomplish this. With a clear destination, you can set your GPS and utilize available tools to facilitate your arrival.

As Habakkuk 2:2 in the Bible says, "Write the vision; make it plain...." Your signature on an insurance policy, and payment of your first premium, can be the start of your wealth-creation strategy. Once you've done so, protect and build your new estate; leverage it; and pass it on—to perpetuate the cycle of generational wealth creation.

If you're not already inspired to take the first step to make insurance the cornerstone of your estate, take a minute to think again about those whom you love and wish to benefit from the assets you will build in life. Doing so makes it easier to shift your perspective on insurance, so that you'll no longer see it as simply one more monthly bill. Even if you don't love anyone, just remember: *You're a million-dollar asset... So what are you doing for yourself? And, what are you doing to contribute to the betterment and enrichment of the Black community?*

IF WE EVER COME TOGETHER: MILLION-DOLLAR-ME ACTION STEP

As a financial-status exercise, immediately review the current life insurance policy or policies that you have in place to see if you have adequate coverage, based on the teachings in this chapter. If not, take action and research options for getting more coverage. And, if you don't have any coverage, don't delay in acquiring it!

Also take this opportunity to calculate the value of your current estate, as described in this chapter, including:

- Your Home
- Retirement Savings
- Checking and Savings Balances
- Investments
- Cars, Collectibles, Jewelry, etc.

Now, add to that total the face value of your life insurance policies. Be sure to step back and fully appreciate the total value that you've calculated as a recognition of where you are, what you've accomplished and earned, and where you are in the life cycle described in Diagram 8. for continuing to build your financial future.

RULE #3. YOU CAN'T EARN YOUR WAY TO WEALTH

BUILDING UPON THE work in the last chapter that showed you how life insurance can help you to establish and control an estate worth millions of dollars, similar to families in communities around us, we will combine that information with the **"4 Paramount Wealth-Building Practices"** outlined in this chapter. These Practices are part of the Untold Rules for Black Prosperity and Legacy. We will use them to help you to establish a roadmap to build, protect, leverage, and pass on wealth. You will see how life insurance is an essential foundation and first step. However, in order to maximize and ensure benefits that contribute to your own—and our overall, collective—empowerment, you must create a comprehensive financial plan built around your specific circumstances. With this plan it will become clear that your earnings, alone, are not enough for you to acquire wealth. If you haven't already, you'll also have to include ownership, equity, investments, property, and inheritance in your estate.

Depending on your age, the "4 Paramount Wealth-Building Practices" can guide you over several decades of your life, and they should be updated as aspects of your life change. Too many of us live our lives reactively, rather than proactively. We get on the hamster wheel of our work and personal lives and just keep going, doing the best we can with what we know.

Maya Angelou once said to Oprah Winfrey, "When you knew better, you did better." Put in the present tense, this advice applies to all of us throughout our entire lives.

WHEN YOU KNEW BETTER, YOU DID BETTER.

Creation of a personal financial-empowerment plan is meant to make you work smarter—not harder—and to make better decisions that are well researched and thought out. Such a plan also becomes a form of financial armor that—once you evaluate risks and rewards—aims to protect you from threats and not leave anything exposed that could potentially wipe you out financially before you reach your long-term goals.

Far too often and for too long, each generation of African-Americans has had to start from scratch—even when the family had made some economic gains. My insurance team and I have seen the losses that occur—sometimes tragically so—when money, property, land, and businesses were not properly protected, invested, or set up (legally and financially) for a smooth transfer to beneficiaries. This includes minimizing taxes and other related penalties. In addition, inadequate planning may result in the *wrong* person ending up with your assets, legal fees burning through the inheritance, or the government repossessing the house or land in question.

We can't continue to have a "just go with the flow" or "take a gamble that things will work out" attitude towards life if we want to radically transform the financial profile of Black families and communities. Too frequently, folks are also leaving it up to chance that their money will build and multiply on its own. Instead, you can begin to live an intentional life by design by using your new attitude and approach to build wealth that can be passed on intergenerationally. By the end of this chapter, you will have a newly minted financial-empowerment plan (grounded in life insurance) that is a living, breathing document that you can use to review your finances periodically. You'll be able to adjust and refresh your wealth-building GPS, so your financial-empowerment plan can generate and spread power and security intergenerationally—and indefinitely.

A NEW MINDSET

A paradigm shift must accompany the creation of your financial-empowerment plan, whereby you look at every "play" and choice you make about your finances offensively or defensively. For instance, you may choose to act defensively by forgoing a fancy new vehicle, fresh off the lot, and opting for a used but reliable one instead, in order to put the money saved towards a down payment to acquire a rental property. Or you may opt to act offensively by buying stock in an initial public offering (IPO) for a hot tech company that is about to go public. This new way of viewing wealth creation means evaluating the timing of major financial decisions and making tough calls when it comes to prioritizing spending.

How does the very nature of our work and the decisions that we make regarding the money we earn align with—or clash against—our financial-empowerment plan? The choices in each of our plans embody our priorities and values. In the first chapter we talked about understanding our value and worth. In the second we learned that, if you have a valuable asset, you should insure it well above its replacement value—and combine it with other financial instruments to create a safety net. In this chapter you will learn, respectively, how to **P**rotect, **P**lan, **P**reserve, and **P**ass along what you've created.

There's also a common-sense aspect to this plan. Would it seem wise, for instance, to invest in a mutual fund when you don't yet have health insurance? Working every day is a means to an end, but ask yourself: To *what* end? It can't be just for paying bills, or to look good and pose in the present. I know we say that we should be building something of value for the future, but our actions don't always follow suit. For example, the fact that some of us continue to make the minimum contributions to our 401(k)s year after year is not helping us to create and work towards a future vision of financial greatness.

We can and should take a page from our ancestors. With the advent of modern-day slavery, Black people became the workhorses of the world, fueling capitalist and colonial expansion. Even in slavery, however, some of our ancestors were strategic and intentional about how they lived their lives—even though somebody else technically *owned* their lives. For example, some got their masters to agree to rent them out to other farms for additional work beyond their daily tasks by crafting a deal that split the rental fee between the owners and themselves. These slaves then leveraged the funds they saved from this fee-splitting arrangement to eventually purchase freedom for them and their families.

If, while enslaved, some of our ancestors were still able to get up and work every day, guided by a long-term vision, then we cannot get up and go to work every day without vision and purpose as well. As Proverbs 29:18 says: *Where there is no vision, the people perish.*

History teaches us great lessons, based on the creativity and persistence of our ancestors, but we don't even need to look that far back: For many of us, our parents were exemplary, too. They knew that if you wanted something you worked harder for it. There's tremendous merit to hard work—and much that comes from it. However, such work needs to be married to strategy and vision in order to have greater value and impact. In addition to saving money for your child's college, are you setting aside enough money for him or her to get tutoring *now*? Is it better for you to help to pay for your child's college degree out of pocket, or to make her take a loan while you continue to contribute towards your retirement fund? These are the types of questions you need to be asking as you craft your financial-empowerment plan. There is no one right answer, but don't keep your head down, mindlessly grinding daily at work and at home. Look up and take careful stock of your future!

Life isn't just about accumulating assets—even though, yes, they visually show that you've made progress. The car, the house, the expensive designer-name acquisitions: those are easy markers to demonstrate your financial and social progress—but they can also be lazy ones. Ask yourself more nuanced questions to figure out if you're really doing *well.* Look for success beyond the tangible.

I am the highest-earning person among my parents and siblings, and—because of my MBA—I'm also the highest educated. However, I often ask myself: Have I *arrived?* Sometimes we think that we're better than or more accomplished than those who came before us due to our education, salary, and buying power. My parents worked government jobs and had peace of mind, confidently knowing that they were not going to get fired tomorrow. I used to work in the corporate sector, where downsizing and rightsizing loom constantly, company loyalty to employees is a thing of the past, and the tradeoff to higher wages is far less job stability.

With the money they earned at their government jobs, my parents paid off their mortgage, bought and sold properties along the way, retired, and live a happy, comfortable, satisfying life. Meanwhile, some of us who earn six figures are nervous about the monthly mortgage payments on our *big* houses, wondering if we're overextended and have purchased more house than we can comfortably afford. Many of us may have more money, but we don't have a safety net that lets us sleep soundly at night.

My English mother was an only child, and my Grenadian father had eight siblings. In his family, my father was always the straight-and-narrow, responsible one. He felt driven to own his own home and purchase rental property that would appreciate and provide him with additional income. The old-school West Indian mentality that you have to live beneath your means, and own things that cannot be taken away from you, guided him. *That* was true freedom. When some members of his family, who exercised less care and wisdom with their finances, came to him for assistance, he didn't feel compelled to be charitable. My father's thinking: They had the same opportunities that he had but had squandered theirs. He had to take care of his own.

I moved to the U.S. from England with my parents when I was a child, and I also inherited my parents' immigrant mindset. As I share my insights on wealth building and financial empowerment with others, I'm trying to impart it to my cousins and other family members of my generation as well—but they don't always receive what I consider to be valuable information in the way that I hope they would. For instance, I had a relative with a chronic health issue who met with a life insurance agent I recommended and managed to get coverage. Not long after, when friends said the policy wasn't a necessary investment, this family member let it lapse—and likely won't be able to obtain coverage again.

As Romans 12:2 says, and so many of us have frequently heard from the pulpit: *Do not conform to the pattern of this world, but be transformed by the renewing of your mind.* If you want to change your financial future, you have to change your mindset. My children are the first generation born in the U.S., and I aim to work hard, maximize what I've earned, and set them up for success—not just monetarily, but by teaching them about good financial stewardship. All of us need to do that for the next generation. This is what this book, and this movement, are all about. We're fighting the good fight in honor of our ancestors and their sacrifices, *and* to actively work to manifest the promises and opportunities that we want the future to hold for our children.

THE WEALTH-BUILDING PYRAMID

The "4 Paramount Wealth-Building Practices" are illustrated in Diagram 9, to help you to grasp the process and steps necessary for building fiscal strength and achieving financial freedom. The pyramid is divided into several layers that correspond with each of the four Practices: Protect, Plan, Preserve, and Pass Along.

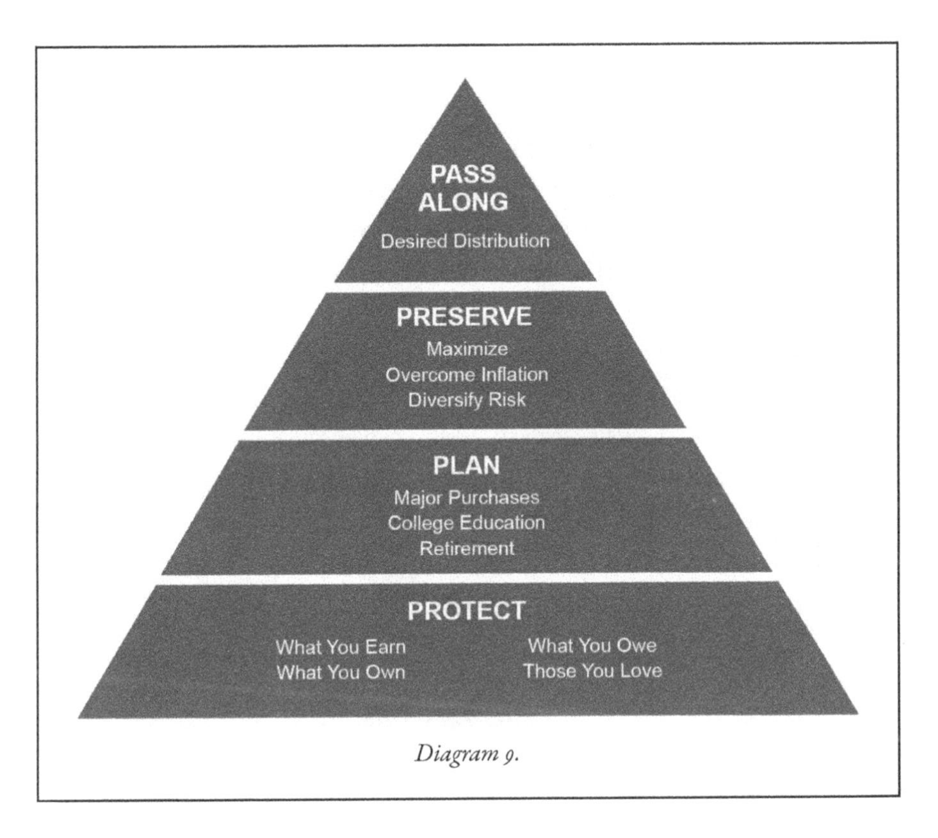

Diagram 9.

As we discuss each layer, I will list financial tools and strategies to consider. They will serve as the framework for the building blocks of your personal financial house. I strongly feel that these life-changing Practices should be taught in schools and colleges, as well as to young people who just got their first jobs and are in the nascent stages of their careers. We also need to conduct refresher reviews of these Practices as we get older, because we must think of the long-term reality of our lives. According to the Social Security Administration's (SSA) website, as of 2017, men have an expected lifespan of 84.3 years and women 86.6 years. And those are just averages. About one out of every four 65-year-olds today will live past age 90, and one out of 10 will live past 95.

This information means that we really need to put a long-term strategy in place to maximize our finances appropriately, and to clearly define our financial goals and destination. Diagram 10 breaks the years of our lives into three sections, with approximate age ranges, two of which combine several of the four Practices together. The first section, ages 1–20, focuses on our school years, a period when most of us are typically not working at all—or not working full-time jobs—so there is no real wealth-building opportunity. However, it is a time in which we can prepare and position ourselves for life, through school, and by determining our desired profession. The latter can help us with the estimated annual salary and income amount that we will use as our base.

The second section, ages 21–65, is the 44-year span during which we are typically working, accumulating assets, building our lives, and getting paid by someone else. This is the time to Protect and Plan our wealth strategy. The third section is the 66–85+ portion, during which you will plan to retire and enjoy the fruits of your labor; for many, this involves a shift to having to pay yourself from investments and savings. Hence, this is the time where we must think about having to Preserve and Pass Along our wealth.

Diagram 10.

Years	*20 years (ages 1–20)*	*44 years (age 21–65)*	*19+ years (age 66–85+)*
Focus	School	Work	Retirement
Wealth Building Practice		**Protect and Plan**	**Preserve and Pass Along**

It's from the perspective of this lifespan continuum—totaling 85+ years—that we need to build each of our financial-empowerment plans. Remember: *We're humans—not hamsters.* We can't just jump on the wheel every day. We need to pause, carefully evaluate, and map out our finances in the form of a plan.

Now let's take a look at the pyramid layers in detail:

WEALTH PRACTICE #1—*PROTECT.*

The base level of the pyramid is where you will begin to **build the foundation for your estate, accompanied by a protection strategy**, usually in your 20s. This will serve as the bedrock upon which you'll continue to construct your wealth for the rest of your life. In many cases, when I talk to individuals and families about their financial plans, this stage is either missing or incomplete. This is the stage at which people should begin looking to **protect what they earn, own, and owe, as well as those they love.** People want to jump to stocks, mutual funds, and other sexy-sounding investments. However, without appropriate protection at the baseline, your whole financial plan is at risk. Those aforementioned financial products should come later.

As you can see from the illustration in Diagram 11, the financial instruments that you *need* at the protection stage (where applicable) are:

Diagram 11.

Health insurance	Savings or checking account
Life insurance	Emergency fund
Disability income insurance	Short-term fund (down payment for your house, car, or family vacation)
Auto insurance	Debt-management plan
Homeowners insurance	Will

Often, during this initial phase of wealth creation, the foundation of the pyramid that's created is too small (not enough coverage or savings) or too loose (all of the instruments listed have not been purchased and/or implemented), and one unexpected change—even a tiny one—can cause the whole pyramid to collapse. As a result, all that you've done to build your finances up will crumble, only leaving behind rubble at the base that you have to salvage through—and use to start again. Use the list I shared as a guide and checklist for yourself.

The underlying purpose of this primary stage where you protect your possessions, is to provide you with a cushion in case of an unexpected event, such as job loss or health issue. If you do not have enough in emergency savings or insurance, chances are that such an event will require you to dig into your long-term savings, borrow, or—worse—suffer with unpaid bills and collections. The first option will undoubtedly deplete what you have saved and jeopardize your distant-horizon goals. The good news: Insurance can bear the burden of such risk, so you don't have to self-fund an emergency. Thus, there is a need for the defensive planning, entailed in the Protect stage of your financial-empowerment plan, in order to safely maintain momentum and continue to build your estate. Specific uses of financial products for this phase are:

- **Life insurance** protects what you *earn*;
- **Health, home, and auto insurance** protect what you *own*, as well as what you *owe* (mortgages, credit cards, etc.);
- **Disability insurance**, a **will**, and **power of attorney** protect *those you love*—yourself included. Disability coverage provides supplementary income in the event of an illness or accident that prevents the insured from working. A will is a legal declaration of a person's wishes regarding the disposal of property after death. A power of attorney allows you to appoint a person or organization to manage your affairs if you become unable to do so;
- **Proper savings and/or a checking account** will help to reduce check cashing and money order fees, and is a better method of tracking spending;
- A **debt-management plan** will assist you in keeping on top of debt payments, your credit rating, and overspending;
- A **short-term fund** serves as a gentle reminder of the goal(s) you're working toward over the next three to six months.

This is how we obtain the kind of sound-sleep financial security that I discussed earlier that still eludes so many of us—even when we're high earners. Having all of these items in place creates a solid foundation for your estate, which we discussed in the last chapter. The Protect stage of wealth building is one that we often forget and fail to see as important. The strength and stability of what you are building depends heavily on this first level. When you are building a skyscraper, the longest stage is digging the foundation. Then, after completing the foundation, everything else happens faster. Do not let your basic security and contingency plan be an afterthought. It must be the mandatory foundation upon which you build *your* financial pyramid.

WEALTH PRACTICE #2—*PLAN.*

This is the portion of your pyramid where you Plan, prioritize, and customize your personal financial-empowerment plan for the wealth that you are accumulating and expanding. Only enter this tier if you have completed and secured the Protect level of the pyramid. If we go by the Social Security Administration lifespan estimate I cited earlier, this second pyramid layer represents roughly a 44-year span. This is where you will be preparing and setting aside funds to finance many of your life milestones: weddings and honeymoons; new babies; homes; education; yearly vacations; launching a business; retirement; and much more. At this phase, you should also be developing your career, preserving your health, and getting your legal affairs in order.

As much as we would love for the Plan phase to financially cover all our heart's desires, most of us probably can't do *everything* we want, so we have to prioritize. This is the time to assess your goals and budget, maintain financial records, and tally your net worth annually to track your progress. You must also align your spending with your income and eliminate and avoid consumer debt. This may be new and daunting, but it gets easier, and—if you choose to work with them—there are professionals who can help you.

To create real and sustainable wealth, it is necessary to *own* things. By this I mean building and accumulating "foundational assets," as shown in Diagram 12, such as a home or rental property, retirement accounts and pensions, college-education funds for children and grandchildren, permanent life insurance, and a small business (for those who are inclined to be in business).

Concentrate your energy on investing in things that routinely increase in value, build equity, and have tax advantages. In my life, I have borrowed in the form of loans, and taken withdrawals from my 401(k) (sometimes with tax penalties), and also sold off some of my foundational assets, in order to further expand my wealth. For instance, I once took out a home-equity loan to buy a second property and to invest in a floral wholesale business with two friends from business school. Other investments to consider at this stage are "speculative assets," e.g., stocks and bonds, commodities (oil, gold, metals, etc.), Real Estate Investment Trusts (REITs), art, and venture capital. Since this latter group of investments will usually have a higher degree of risk—typically associated with instruments with a potentially higher rate of return—I suggest that you seek a financial advisor for these options.

Diagram 12. Savings and investments vehicles

Foundational assets	*Speculative assets*
Primary home	Stocks
Retirement and pension funds	Bonds
College-education funds	Commodities
Permanent life insurance	REITS
Rental property	Art
Small business	Venture capital

As you focus on your major life purchases and saving for both college education and retirement, I want to bring special attention and urgency to the fact that Blacks still set aside a lot less for retirement in the form of 401(k)s and IRAs (also called defined-contribution plans—meaning you have to pay into it yourself, as opposed to defined-benefit plans like pensions), as compared to Whites. For decades, these voluntary retirement plans have been replacing traditional employee pensions in the majority of companies, and even in what once seemed to be their final stronghold: government jobs. The focus for companies and institutions is on cutting employer costs. According to the website benefitspro.com, African-Americans are also confronted by the following factors:

1. **Lower overall use of employer-sponsored plans:** In 2013, only 41% of African-American families had retirement savings accounts, versus 65% of White, non-Hispanic families.
2. **Lower levels of plan enrollment and contribution rates:** Approximately 69% of African-Americans enrolled in such plans, versus 79% of Whites. And Blacks had contribution rates that were 22.2% lower than those of their White counterparts.
3. **Unfavorable demographic, economic, and work-related factors:** Compared to their White peers, the average African-American plan participant is 14% younger, has 10% less job tenure, earns an average salary that is 30% lower, and has a 28.4% higher job turnover rate.

The end result of participating less, and having accumulated less, is that Black families are left standing on shakier ground during what should be their Golden Years. The 2013 Federal Reserve Bank's "Survey of Consumer Finances" places the racial disparity gap between the average Black family's retirement savings—in 401(k)s, 403(b)s, and IRAs—when compared to that of Whites at over $110,000 (see Diagram 13).

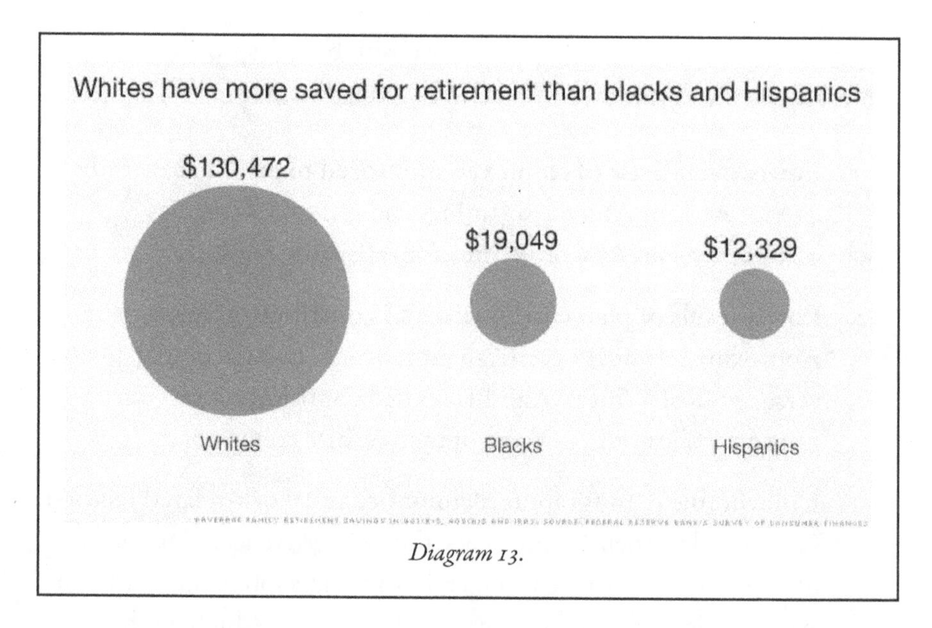

Diagram 13.

I say all of this to encourage you to make this investment in your own retirement a priority, especially if your job gives you the option to match your contribution (average company-match ranges can go as high as 5% of your annual salary). You should see this as additional earnings due to you, and not leave that money on the table because you didn't invest back into yourself. I also want to advise you to make use of any and all retirement calculators and resources available to you through your benefits department. Take the necessary time and effort to understand your time horizon and expected payout in retirement.

Another point to consider when investing your money during your "Plan" phase is to be mindful of not making too many purchases of depreciating assets (such as a high-end car you can't effortlessly afford) and symbols of wealth that may provide momentary pleasure or status, but ultimately rob you—and your family—of wealth creation. At this juncture, your simple mandate is to save money and grow the assets you've accumulated.

While I am not suggesting that you can't spoil yourself every now and then, or that your life must be all about deprivation, with no room for celebration, this entire financial exercise is designed to get you to start employing a financial strategy. Ultimately, having a vision and an accompanying strategic plan will allow you to have the life you want and to maintain security and stability for yourself and future generations. You'll still enjoy life—there's no need to become a monk—but just recognize there will have to be tradeoffs. The greater security that comes from making smart sacrifices will make life sweeter.

This is also the part of your life cycle where you can begin to make the kind of investments that I advised you against making during the Protect phase of the pyramid. You can now start to become creative and to think outside the box when it comes to investments, and you can uncover ways to still meet your goals—while decreasing risk. For instance, instead of purchasing an investment property (which has a mixture of both glory and potential headaches, like non-paying tenants), buy shares in a REIT, an alternative investment that allows you to own a share in an investment property and reap much of the upside without doing all of the work entailed in directly owning such a property.

You should also be focused on your primary residence and examine your motives for renting versus owning. Are you viewing renting as simply a means to an end—for instance, living in a studio or sharing an apartment with several roommates to keep expenses down, while stashing away money to buy a home? Or are you renting just to be able to say you live in a really nice place, in a hip part of a metropolitan area (meanwhile, you're spending more than 50% of your take-home salary, with no discretionary income left over to begin constructing your wealth-building pyramid)? Are you aware of the tax benefits of home ownership, as well as the many programs available to first-time homebuyers who qualify? Really do your due diligence on all of your financial decisions.

Lastly, I have to note that business ownership is an opportunity to build wealth, as a business can both potentially appreciate and provide tax advantages—whether it's home-based, online, or brick and mortar.

I also want you to be mindful of some of the common pitfalls at this stage of your financial journey. I'll offer two notes of caution: 1) Responsibly manage debt and credit, as both can become major detractors and time killers in your wealth accumulation; and 2) Maintain perseverance and resilience through the ups and downs your life's journey. I offer this advice after having had personal experiences on both fronts. I am fortunate to have had a lot of professional and personal successes, but I have also had my share of heartbreak, hard times, financial losses, and sacrifice.

The first story I'll share has to do with ruining my credit score by taking off to travel to South Africa and throughout Europe in my early 20s. I landed a modeling contract that I leveraged to see many new parts of the world I'd never seen. Initially thinking I'd only be away a few months, my travels turned into an exciting two-year tour. However, while being featured in commercials, magazines, and on runways was an amazing experience, I neglected to pay any of my bills and credit cards back at home. The sporadic modeling jobs I was getting were good, but only covered my expenses while I was away.

So when I did finally return to the U.S., having expanded and grown my social life, I found my entire financial life was in default and my credit scores were embarrassingly low. I then had to dig myself out of a massive self-inflicted hole before I could even start rebuilding. I had to negotiate with all of my creditors, set up repayment plans, and then obtain a secured credit card because no one was willing to lend to me. After that experience, it really hit home when I heard Rev. Dr. DeForest "Buster" Soaries, Jr. speak at several of his conferences that I attended (promoting his debt-management program and book, *Dfree: Breaking Free from Financial Slavery*), where he quoted Proverbs 22:7, "The rich rule over the poor, and the borrower is slave to the lender." It made me reminisce about the colossal mistake I had made—and how I vowed never to put myself in that position again.

It literally took several years to reestablish my credit worthiness, with lots being spent on late fees and high interest rates—not to mention the inconvenience. I was at the mercy of these companies that held my future in their hands as they decided whether or not they would extend the credit necessary to allow me to rebuild my credit score and reestablish myself. If you have fallen down a similar hole, consider signing up for the Dfree program. Also research the great initiatives available through the Hope Centers, created by John Hope Bryant. Both can help you to build back up your tarnished credit to a sterling 750 score (I highlight both programs in the Resources section at the end of this book).

I'm going to share another very personal and somewhat painful story that I hope can guide you on how to cope in times when even the best-laid plans go awry. The saying, "Man plans, and God laughs," comes to mind here. I previously mentioned that I was a partner in a not-so-small wholesale floral business venture. I had hastily entered into it with my two friends from business school because it seemed like a great opportunity. It had pretty much broken even in its first two years and was on track to turn a hefty profit the third year when the Great Recession of 2008 hit. During that time, items like flowers were seen as a luxury that people opted not to purchase in hard times. Then, the fuel surcharges from the flower growers (many of them oversees) got passed back to us for the deliveries.

All of that, coupled with the additional fuel cost to run the five delivery trucks that we operated, added to our rapidly growing debt. Add to that the multiple business liabilities (for which we had given personal guarantees), including our not-so-well-negotiated monthly lease with our shop's landlord. The owner refused to let us out of the lease even as our business was going under. As if all of that were not difficult enough, I was simultaneously juggling my full-time corporate job. I had a failing entrepreneurial endeavor on the side that my partners and I couldn't easily sell in a recession. So to stop the hemorrhaging, we had to sell off some of the business assets and lay off our dedicated flower shop employees.

My personal life also took a tremendous hit during that time. I had borrowed against my home, taking out a home equity loan to invest in the business. I had exhausted my credit cards to support both the business and my family, all the while accumulating more and more debt. The entire situation—both personally and professionally—contributed to mounting stress in my marriage. Ultimately, we were forced to sell our big suburban home (which we had overstretched to purchase at the height of the market) at a significant loss. Not wanting to accept failure, file for bankruptcy, or take the ego blow tied to my position as someone who espoused sound financial planning as my career, yet was struggling financially myself, I decided to commit myself to years of sacrifice to get back on track—and a sacrifice it was, indeed.

My then-wife (now ex-wife) and I downsized to a two-bedroom apartment in Harlem with our two kids. We shuffled and staggered our bill payments, and we cut out all unnecessary spending, including date nights, expensive presents, family vacations, and so on. We basically lived like we were broke. After several years, we filed for divorce. It took additional time after that before I began to see financial daylight again. Looking back at the situation, I had veered so far off course from what, and how, I had planned things: I had acquired a great corporate job and a beautiful home; I was an entrepreneur with a small business; I'd demonstrated responsibility and sound financial planning and made investments; and suddenly large chunks of those accomplishments were undone. It had all gone out the window with a catastrophic economic downturn that was completely outside of my control.

But even during this time of darkness and despair, I remember thinking that, while I was derailed and disrupted, I'd not been completely devastated. I thanked God every day that I still had my high-paying corporate job to cover my bills and maintain my household. I still had some foundational assets—rental properties in both New York City and Miami (both of which also lost value at the time), my 401(k) (against which I had already taken loans), and life insurance (which I continued to pay faithfully, regardless of my financial hardships). With deep reflection and insight, I realized that life is easy in the great times, but it takes real leadership, fortitude, and sacrifice in the hard times.

The fact that I had a solid financial foundation to fall back on really made a difference, and it allowed me to be down, but not out. I hope you'll see this as yet another reason I say to set money aside and to build your cushion, as doing so will help you to maintain the resilience and perseverance necessary to stay the course and will offset the inevitable and unforeseen circumstances that hit you unexpectedly.

With these tools, strategies, and words of caution in mind, you have 44 years to build with the goal of, not simply having enough to preserve you through your golden years, but of having an estate healthy enough to give you the flexibility to actually enjoy that phase of your life. Time moves fast—so focus on setting money aside. The sooner you start, the better off you'll be in the long run. Make your money work for you. Invest wisely and diversify your investments, and—if need be—don't be afraid to reach out to a professional financial advisor for help.

"DO I SAVE FOR MY RETIREMENT OR MY CHILD'S COLLEGE EDUCATION?"

A common question all families ask—particularly those in the Black community who want to set their children on a better path than they had—is whether or not to prioritize saving for retirement or for their children's college education. As a parent, I know that you want the best for your children, and that your instincts probably lean toward saving for their higher education. However, although many students delay their matriculation or drop out altogether because of funding challenges, it's helpful to remember that, while you can borrow to pay for college, you cannot take out a loan to cover your retirement.

So my answer is that parents should favor saving for retirement over saving for their children's college educations. According to a 2016 *Time* magazine article titled, "1 in 3 Americans has saved $0 for retirement," the reality is that 56 percent of American workers have less than $10,000 saved for the latter years of their lives. There is also a concern that Social Security might not be as viable and reliable a support option for retirement income in the future as it once was. Because of these reasons, it's critical that you start saving for your own retirement as soon as possible. The urgency here is to take advantage of compounded interest growing and multiplying your money over as long a time as possible. A 10-year delay in starting to save can have a significant impact on the amount accumulated. Following this same train of thought, if you choose to focus on educational costs, you will spend your money on your children's college enrollment first, before starting to contribute to your nest egg, so there won't be as much time for your retirement savings to compound. So when you do retire, you'll be getting less bang for your buck!

In order to free up money to put toward saving for a sufficient nest egg, when planning for your child's higher education, look to alternatives that won't necessarily compete with your retirement savings. You might consider a 529 savings plan, which is a fund that can grow, tax-deferred, and can receive contributions from relatives. Proceeds from a 529 have to be applied to qualified higher education expenses in order to be tax-advantaged. Thanks to the 2017 tax overhaul, 529s can also be used for private elementary tuition as well.

Here are some other options for you to consider when it gets closer to college time:

1. **Stay in state**—You can typically cut your costs almost in half by selecting an in-state, versus out-of-state, college. Similar savings can occur when comparing public colleges to private colleges.
2. **Max out financial aid**—Be sure to investigate all your options, starting with free sources of funding, such as scholarships, endowments, and grants. Once those are exhausted, your next step may be to consider low-cost student loans.
3. **Attend a junior college**—It is usually cheaper to have your child attend a local junior or community college for a year or two, then transfer to a four-year university to finish up his or her degree. Most state universities accept junior college credits, and acceptance is sometimes easier than it is for students applying in high school.
4. **Share the load**—While you may believe that it is your responsibility to pick up the entire tab, there is no shame in asking grandparents and other relatives to help with the cost. Also, many financial experts recommend making sure your children have some skin in the game and contribute a portion as well, perhaps working on campus.
5. **Use your other financial tools**—Remember that we discussed borrowing against the cash value of a whole life insurance policy,

Don't forget that when you change jobs, assuming that you have a 401(k) in your current position, you have the option of moving your account into your new employer's 401(k) or rolling it over into an individual retirement account (IRA).

Retirement is another time when you can make the switchover from your 401(k) to an IRA. Consolidating your accounts is a great way to keep track of them. An IRA also offers several noteworthy features, such as having a larger universe of investment choices. A Roth IRA requires you to make your contributions using after-tax income, which can benefit you if you believe you will be in a higher tax bracket when you begin taking distributions, or if general tax rates may be higher by the time you retire (a traditional IRA taxes you when you take money out as distributions). If you had the ability to borrow from your old 401(k) account, you may lose that ability if you roll over to a traditional IRA; however, a Roth IRA will allow you to maintain this feature.

Lastly, upon your death, there's a good chance that your 401(k) will be paid in one lump sum to your beneficiary. IRAs have more payout options to reduce the possible tax implications that come with a lump sum payout. You can gain additional sources of income from the sale of the other assets you accumulated in the Plan stage of your life. Many people sell their primary homes to downsize into something smaller, like a condo, creating an additional reservoir of cash. Money from the sale of other foundational and speculative assets can be rolled over into other long-term, guaranteed investments like annuities. Be sure to consider speaking with your financial and tax advisors to assess tax implications from any asset sale.

Once in retirement, it's best that you cover your basic living expenses with guaranteed lifetime income. You can then invest the rest of your portfolio to protect against inflation. And don't forget to have a plan for long-term care. Lastly, while preserving wealth is the underlying message of this section, be sure that you are also enjoying this stage of life. Whether you treat yourself to a new car, condo, start a business, or travel the world—you've earned it!

"DO I USE MY MONEY FOR RETIREMENT, OR SAVE IT AS AN INHERITANCE FOR MY CHILDREN?"

As 78 million Baby Boomers are marching headlong and headstrong into retirement, many of them are discussing how much money they should leave for their kids. As the Millennial generation moves out of the house and into the real world, many Boomers are looking to leave a little something to their children and grandchildren.

The best advice I've heard to answer the question, "Do I use my money for retirement, or save it as an inheritance for my children?" comes from retirement-planning guru, Tom Hegna. He says, "Do not leave your kids or grandkids any money. I repeat, do NOT leave your kids or grandkids any money! Set up a life insurance policy to leave a legacy, so that you can spend pennies and your heirs will get dollars."

WEALTH PRACTICE #4—*PASS ALONG.*

This is the top of the pyramid, and it **focuses on detailing your wishes for the distribution of your remaining wealth and assets and ensuring that you create a financial legacy that can be passed along to those you love.** Your empowerment plan will now incorporate components like a will, estate planning, creating a trust, and structured charitable gifting. To help strategize and implement, you should consider questions like:

- **How do you want to be remembered when you pass?** For instance, do you want to further the educations of students at your HBCU alma mater, give to your church, or create a family foundation? (HBCUs are Historically Black Colleges and Universities.)
- **Have you made provisions for succession planning and continuation of the business you own?** There are savvy ways to do so that avoid the tax problems that are often so prevalent when settling estates. I've come across enough cases of million-dollar brownstones and thousand-acre farms that were lost due to

> defaulted taxes that I don't want to see it happen to others—and especially not to *you*. Your objective is to incorporate an estate plan that will permit the tax-efficient transfer of assets to heirs and/or favorite causes.

In addition to a financial advisor, an estate attorney can be essential at this stage to ensure that you take the proper steps to look after your loved ones. This is especially important in the LGBTQ community, as many states do not recognize same-sex unions—which are distinct from *married* gay couples, which is federally recognized. Chapter 6 will provide more on this topic of estate planning, including *Advanced-Planning* strategies around structuring your will, trust, and taxes on your terms.

YOUR PERSONAL FINANCIAL GPS

The nice thing about following the "4 Paramount Wealth-Building Practices" method for building your personal financial-empowerment plan is that you will begin with a solid financial foundation upon which to build. Then, as you get older and more sophisticated, you journey to the top of the pyramid to address the higher financial needs you will have later in life. This method goes beyond any one product, company, or strategy. The plan you will create can serve as your personal financial GPS throughout your life. Review it regularly, and update your plan as your life changes. Check off the products and layers as you progress and grow. Take time to plan the milestones of your 85+ years using this tried-and-true structure. Most importantly: Get started today!

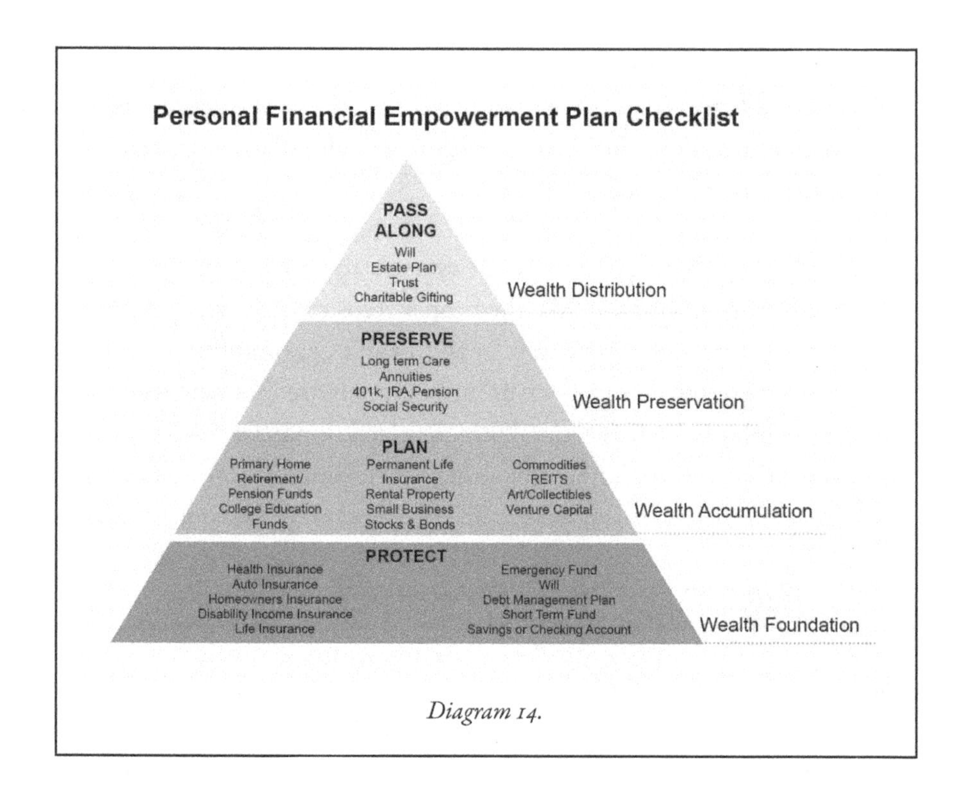
Personal Financial Empowerment Plan Checklist
PASS ALONG
Will
Estate Plan
Trust
Charitable Gifting
Wealth Distribution
PRESERVE
Long term Care
Annuities
401k, IRA,Pension
Social Security
Wealth Preservation
PLAN
Primary Home
Retirement/
Pension Funds
College Education
Funds
Permanent Life
Insurance
Rental Property
Small Business
Stocks & Bonds
Commodities
REITS
Art/Collectibles
Venture Capital
Wealth Accumulation
PROTECT
Health Insurance
Auto Insurance
Homeowners Insurance
Disability Income Insurance
Life Insurance
Emergency Fund
Will
Debt Management Plan
Short Term Fund
Savings or Checking Account
Wealth Foundation

Diagram 14.

IF WE EVER COME TOGETHER: MILLION-DOLLAR-ME ACTION STEP

Start strategizing your personal financial empowerment plan today using the pyramid checklist in Diagram 14. Remember: You can't earn your way to wealth—you must include ownership, equity, investments, and inheritance in your estate. Be intentional and detailed in mapping out your plan. Even consider including photos and creating a vision board of the type of house, retirement, and business you would like to have for yourself, as well as the ideal college for your children. Be sure to include desired timeframes in your life for these acquisitions. Start at the beginning, and consider which stage of life you are in to answer the following questions:

- **Protect:** Have you protected yourself? Have you protected those you cherish?
- **Plan:** Have you solidified a plan of action, something codified that you and your loved ones can refer to and rely on?
- **Preserve:** Have you adequately put mechanisms in place to preserve what you have built?
- **Pass Along:** Have you taken steps to make sure that your legacy is intact—and that those who you leave behind won't get *left behind* when you pass on?

As also suggested in this chapter, calculate your net worth at least annually to measure and track your progress toward your plan and wealth accumulation. Use the accompanying personal-net-worth statement in Diagram 15 as your guide for monitoring your gains in property value, retirement savings, etc. Add such information in the assets section of the worksheet. Also, in the liabilities section, be mindful of credit card debt, student loans, and borrowing from your home equity, which may slow down your ability to build wealth.

Personal Net Worth Statement

Assets

Cash

Checking/Savings accounts	______
CDs (certificates of deposit)	______
Life Insurance (cash surrender value)	______
Other cash	______

Investments

Securities (stocks, bonds, mutual funds)	______
Treasury Bills	______
College Education Funds ______	
Other Investments	______

Property

Primary Home (market value)	______
Automobile (present value)	______
Jewelry, Art and Collectibles	______
Rental/Other Property	______

Retirement

Retirement accounts (IRA, 401k)	______
Employer Pensions	______
Other Assets	______

Small Business

Small Business (market value)	______
Notes and Accounts receivable	______

Total Assets ______

Liabilities

Real Estate Mortgages	______
Home Equity Loans	______
Auto Loans	______
Credit Card Debt	______
Consumer Loans or Installments	______
Loans on Life Insurance	______
Student Loans	______
Retirement account Loans ______	
Unpaid Taxes	______
Money Owed to Others	______
Small business loans	______
Small business accounts payable	______
Other Liabilities	______

Total Liabilities ______

Net Worth

Total Assets – Total Liabilities ______

Diagram 15.

RULE #4. IF YOU HAVE A LANDLORD *AND* A LEXUS—THEN YOU HAVE A PROBLEM

SO NOW YOU know your worth, have created a hedge of protection around your financial goals through insurance, and established an overarching strategic roadmap to get to your financial destination points. Next, you must evaluate your day-to-day cash flow spending and investing habits, to make sure that they align with your goals, and then implement any necessary changes to ensure their success.

I want to go beyond the concept of a simple budget—which is usually driven by an itemized list of your monthly bills—to instead assess the right amount you should be spending in the various categories of your financial life. For most of us, this process must also be accompanied by a change in our mindset and spending habits. This includes examining whether you are making good financial decisions, assessing whether you are living above or below your means, and determining the areas where you can increase or cut back on your spending. In addition, as you get older and have a family, you must be mindful of shifting priorities within the family unit.

For many of us in the Black community, another Untold Rule that we have not been taught pertains to the *spending guidelines* for our respective incomes and the appropriate percentage allocations for our expenses.

There are *seemingly* random suggestions we hear in life, such as 3% of your salary should go to your 401(k) and 10% toward tithing at your church, and that the bank will only consider a maximum of 33% from your gross salary to apply toward a mortgage payment. That said, what should you do with your remaining income? Are your current spending habits the best they can be?

I realized that, without guidelines, we're more likely to overspend in some areas and under spend in others. If we can find the money to pay for items, then we can fool ourselves into believing that all our financial choices are legitimate and justifiable. We must remember that there is a fundamental difference between the ability to purchase an item and being able to *afford* it. Whether you can purchase the $2,500 designer purse or lease the luxury vehicle for $700 per month is a less relevant point than whether you *should* spend your cash flow this way. This is particularly true if you have to plan for future expenses, like your children's college education, retirement contributions, and making sure your rainy-day umbrella is adequately funded. More often than not, most of us fail to challenge ourselves as to whether what we're spending our money on is what we *should* be spending our money on. The problem is that this lack of introspection and awareness keeps us mired in mere financial existence, rather than propelling us toward our thriving, long-term economic success.

THERE IS A FUNDAMENTAL DIFFERENCE BETWEEN THE ABILITY TO PURCHASE AN ITEM AND BEING ABLE TO AFFORD IT.

After many years of hearing my parents say that I was overspending on things that I gave little thought to—like eating out, clothing, and Christmas gifts—I decided to look at how and what they were seeing. It was eye opening. Later, I went beyond my own spending and took time to investigate how—and why—some people continually live from paycheck to paycheck. What I learned from analyzing their spending were lessons on how to live more frugally and sensibly that I then began to apply to my own life. I also looked at the opportunity cost of making certain decisions to spend and shop, rather than invest. An opportunity cost occurs when you choose to allocate your money towards a particular purchase or investment, making it no longer available once an equally attractive or better purchase or investment opportunity comes along.

Let's take a look at short-term budgeting guidelines, long-term strategies, and opportunity-cost comparisons.

SHORT-TERM AND EVERYDAY-SPENDING PERCENTAGE GUIDELINES

To properly develop your personal budget, and answer questions you may have for yourself—like, "What should I be spending for food, clothing, housing, and my day-to-day living needs?"—you must start by determining the net income that you bring home *after* government deductions—but before voluntary deductions (e.g., 401(k), pension, or other savings contributions). Then, take a close look at what you're currently spending so that you can compare it to families across America in your same income bracket. From there, begin to think about how to better allocate your money using the suggested spending ranges in the accompanying "Budgeting Guidelines" breakdown.

The consumer expenditure categories shown in the Diagram 16 pie chart come from the 2017 U.S. Department of Labor's Bureau of Labor Statistics Consumer Expenditures survey. The information reflects the average percentage of net household income that Americans are currently spending on each of the expense categories. It's important to note that this may not accurately reflect what is realistically affordable for every household.

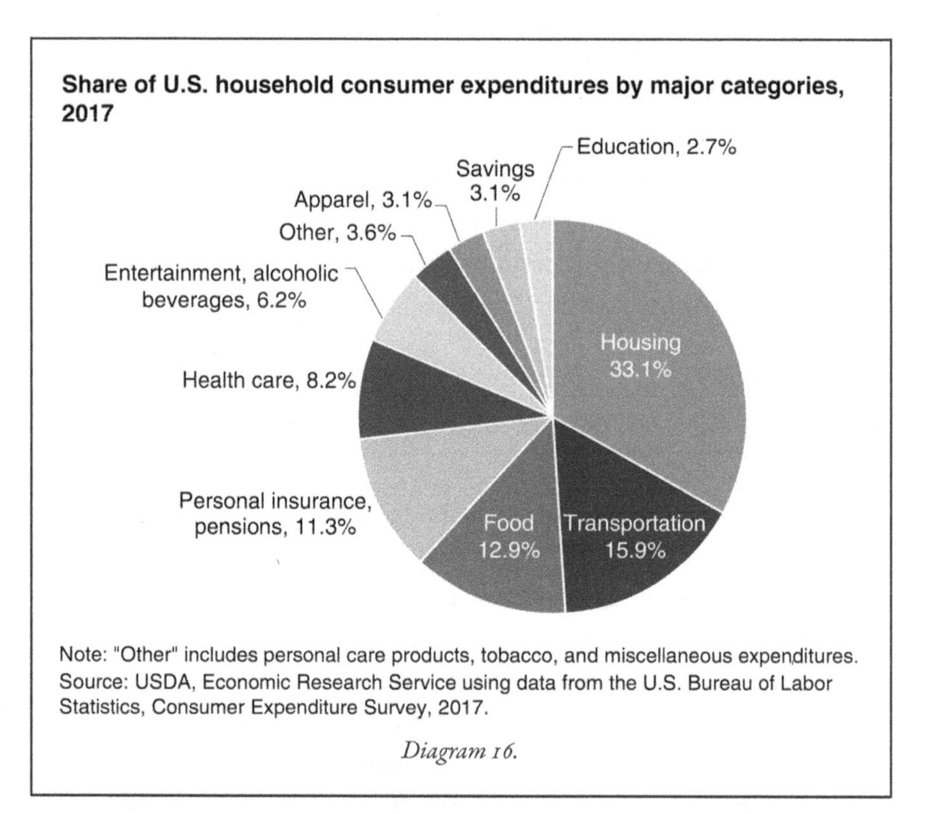

Diagram 16.

In the following section you will see an expansion of the categories listed on the chart, with a more detailed breakdown of the items included. I've also included a broader recommendation of percentage allocations for you to consider. Since the U.S. Department of Labor's Bureau of Labor Statistics showed actual expenditures made by families across the country, yours may vary depending on your particular situation. However, I do want you to look at your largest expenditures in the areas of housing, transportation, food, entertainment, and apparel. Start to consider whether you should put more into savings and debt payments. And once a particular debt is paid off, take the same monthly dollar amount you used to allocate to pay off that debt and deposit it into a savings account instead. Also evaluate whether or not you should spend less on discretionary items. I'll explain more in the sections that follow.

BUDGETING GUIDELINES:

- **Housing: 25–32%**
  This covers rent, mortgage payments—including principal, interest, taxes, and insurance (PITI), a second mortgage, any association dues, and maintenance and repair fees.

  Hint: Don't get in over your head. That's what led to the subprime mortgage crisis that helped to topple the U.S.—and much of the global—economy, when people couldn't pay their mortgages because they had borrowed more than they could afford.

- **Utilities: 5–10%**
  Electricity, heat, water, landline or cell phone, cable and satellite, Internet coverage, and garbage and sewage fees all fall under this category.

  Hint: These really can be just the basic utilities; consider dropping upgrades and premium services, etc.

- **Food: 10–15%**
  Place groceries, dining out, work lunches, school lunches, snacks, convenience-store purchases, and on-the-go beverages like coffee under this category.

  Hint: Less eating out and more home-cooked meals can save a chunk of money.

- **Transportation: 10–15%**
  Place automobile payments, insurance, gas, maintenance and repairs, parking fees, registration, and any parking tickets under this category.

  Hint: Consider less flash in any mode of transportation you lease or own, just keep it good and reliable instead. Remember: If you have a landlord *and* a Lexus—then you have a problem. It's a wealth-building strategy that simply doesn't add up.

- **Clothing: 3–5%**
  This percentage range covers *all* members of the family—and includes dry cleaning, alterations, and repairs.

  Hint: We all love looking great, but consider less floss, and focus on just being neat and presentable. Style isn't about name brands; it's about the unique, signature way in which you put yourself together.

- **Healthcare/Medical: 3–5%**
  Healthcare premiums, copays, prescriptions, over-the-counter medications, deductibles, counseling fees, eyecare, dental, spend-down amounts, and specialists are housed under this category.

  Hint: You *must* have these, because your health is one of your greatest assets—so don't skimp here.

- **Personal and Discretionary: 5–10%**
  Place tithing and charitable giving, entertainment, recreation, tobacco and alcohol, gaming, haircuts, hobbies, and miscellaneous spending here.

  Hint: This is an area largely made up of wants, not needs, so be particularly mindful not to exceed the percentage ranges for this Budgeting Guidelines category.

- **Pensions/401(k)/Life Insurance/Savings: 5–15%**
  This includes out-of-pocket retirement contributions, life insurance, investments, and savings.

  Hint: This is where you should consider increasing your investments—unless you want to work into your 90s.

- **Debt Payments: 5–10%**

  This includes unsecured loans, debt payments (e.g., credit cards), personal debts, education, and emergency savings.

Hint: Keep at the forefront of your mind that your credit impacts your long-term wealth-building opportunities, so be sure to manage your debt and the timeliness of your payments.

Let's put these broad descriptions of common spending into perspective by applying them to the annual earnings of a theoretical dual-income family in order to see the recommended percentages for each category on a monthly basis. Our fictional family of four earns $75,000 per year in New York, with a 26% average tax rate, according to the 2018 Tax Tables.

Annual income:	*$ 75,000*
Net annual income after 26% tax rate:	*$ 55,500*
Net income per month:	***$ 4,500***

Diagram 17. Monthly Expenses

Housing	32%	$ 1,480
Utilities	10%	$ 463
Food	11%	$ 509
Transportation	15%	$ 694
Clothing	3%	$ 139
Healthcare	5%	$ 231
Entertainment	5%	$ 231
401(k)/Insurance	9%	$ 416
Debt	10%	$ 463

By looking at these numbers, you can see how quickly money gets spent. This category breakdown vividly illustrates how making large purchases, splurging, or failing to keep track can skew these suggested limits significantly—and throw an entire budget out of whack.

Let's do an even deeper analysis. Many people find that their budget is quite tight because of their monthly debt payments. The average U.S. household debt is $16,883 for credit cards, $29,539 for auto loans, and $50,626 for student loans, according to the NerdWallet personal-finance website and the Federal Reserve as of 2016. Collectively, these payments often exceed the 5–10% recommended budget allotment for debt payments and take away from contributions to savings and investments. These payments can get even larger as folks make payments late and accumulate additional fees—which potentially includes an increase in interest rate(s). Those who are unbanked and underbanked in our community, and rely on local check-cashing establishments or unscrupulous moneylenders, are often the hardest hit in such a scenario.

We also need to place a microscope on the utilities category, where our combined phone, cable, electric, and gas bill payments, can hit our budgetary limit very quickly when we fail to take the time to explore extra charges. Such charges can be due to unlimited data packages, premium channels, and not being mindful of wasteful or extravagant electricity and heating usage. Upgrading to the newest version of a cell phone and adding the financing cost to your phone bill can further compound such costs.

Similar ways in which small costs can quickly snowball are things like paying $10 per day for lunch at work or spending $5 for Starbucks coffee every morning. These two seemingly simple spends, alone, will total $75 for the week and $300 by month's end—representing nearly 3/5 of this family's food budget. Another shocker is seeing the cost of the fashionable new $480 Fendi belt that a teenager may want to purchase to impress his classmates. That acquisition alone is more than three times the monthly clothing budget allocated for this *entire* family and nearly a third of what that household spends on rent.

For me—and for a number of us—another category that significantly impacts my budget and spending capacity is my child-support payment. I actually pay out several thousand dollars every month, but in looking at the spending chart I noted that there was not a pre-assigned placeholder for this expense. However, I am mindful to include it and aware of it as a priority—as it should be for all who are in the same situation.

WHERE ARE YOU?

How do your expenses compare to the national averages identified above? Does your spending exceed these suggestions? Do you actually *exceed* the 100% category expenditure—which means that you are spending more than you are making (i.e., using and increasing your debt and/or credit cards above your income ability)? Take time to compare the chart to your own financial situation and start thinking of where you can make adjustments to balance your budget.

There are no hard-and-fast rules for family spending, because income levels and family dynamics will vary from house to house. What's reasonable for one family may seem unreasonable to another. Still, for families and individuals just getting started on budgeting, the aforementioned guidelines can be helpful as they provide a formulaic foundation upon which one can introduce financial discipline and rigor.

After reviewing where you stand, I hope that you have been inspired to think of how you can make some adjustments. First, add in and account for expenditures that you have that may not already be covered in the Budgeting Guidelines—such as the child support that I noted above.

Next, start to really think of how you can reallocate your budget for better results— keeping purpose, priority, and proper placement of your money in mind, without spending more money than you already have. If you have expenses such as high-debt payments, childcare, or school expenses, you will need to reduce your spending in other areas to accommodate those higher expenses. This guideline is only a starting point. Based on your income and individual or family circumstances, your allocations may be very different.

Lastly, think about how you can cut back and spend even less. Pay down or pay off some high-interest debt to eliminate those monthly expenses, and then combine the payments previously allocated to those expenses to make larger payments on the remaining debts in order to pay them off even faster. This requires true discipline. Also consider scaling back on entertainment and personal spending on things like coffee, hair and nails, shiny new gadgets, and gratuitous shopping. Remember: *Temporary sacrifices will position you for long-term success!*

CARRYING THROUGH FOR THE LONG TERM

A couple things come to mind when I think about applying these calculations for both short- and long-term planning: First, you should be sure to include all income and special one-time expenses that may arise throughout the year. This includes the things beyond your paycheck, like lump-sum tax refunds and work bonuses, and the subsequent spending that accompanies those lump-sum amounts. For example, during the housing bubble several years ago, some of us refinanced our home mortgages and siphoned off cash to make repairs and other investments.

The unfortunate reality for many Americans who refinanced their mortgages or took out home equity loans is that they used the cash for things like shopping sprees and vacations. When this excess money and these lump sum payments are not captured and recorded in a budget, such spending quickly gets forgotten or erroneously processed in our brains as *free money.* For many of us who participated in the latter area of spending, we were saddled with a lot more debt from acquiring additional depreciating assets that we really didn't need in the first place.

Instead of a spending spree or actually treating yourself in the present, how about a future-focused perspective where you take your lump-sum tax refund, save it, and then combine it with *next* year's refund so that you have enough to put 3% towards a down payment on a new home as a first-time home buyer? Or, better yet, save up until you are able to put 20% down to avoid having to purchase costly private mortgage insurance (PMI). PMI is a monthly fee that gets added to mortgage payments for most home buyers who can't put 20% down. Can you imagine what that celebration will be like as you sit in your new home, reflecting on the sacrifices you made to get there, and the generous reward you've reaped as a result? Who knew budgeting could be so exciting and empowering! I say that only half tongue-in-cheek, but seriously: *Each time you save, celebrate it.* Reward yourself when you achieve a milestone, perhaps with an item from your short-term fund goal(s) list. Such items are ones that you are working toward obtaining within three to six months.

I remember smiling from ear to ear for weeks as I slept on a blow-up mattress, with no other furniture, in the first condo that I'd purchased, on Miami Beach, when I was 28 years old. I used my tax return and the leftover money from my student loan toward the 3% down payment as a first-time home buyer. That sense of accomplishment and ownership kept me on Cloud 9 for a long time. Even though I was scraping to get by managing my bills, that condo turned out to be one of the best investments I've made in my life, and I still own it. I think about how its increasing value has been a blessing and how, in contrast, I have nothing to show for all of the clothes, cars, and partying I spent money on back then. That condo was obviously a much better choice based on the rental income I've received over the years, the mortgage and tax deductions from which I've benefitted, and the times that I've stayed there to enjoy all that South Beach has to offer. And let's not forget that it has significantly increased in value. You can do this, too!

The second long-term consideration for you to think about is how your overall income and expenses add up over time. With the family in our previous scenario, earning $75,000 a year for 20 years (of *uninterrupted* income) totals $1.5 million earned. If this theoretical family had a lump-sum amount of $1.5 million, they may actually want to allocate that money more strategically over the 20 years by asking themselves the following:

- How much of that million-and-a-half should go into our home?
- How much toward our retirement fund?
- How much do we want to put toward our kids' college funding?
- How much do we want to use to underwrite the cost of memorable vacations?

The point here is that lots of "mini-spends" over time don't become shocking to acknowledge until individuals and families take the time to add them up and see the total amount that they have spent on purchases like clothes and entertainment. If they were to think in terms of total spend, then these items will likely take a back seat to more important, impactful purchases or investments. From this assessment, they can also determine how much money they want to put toward necessary or unnecessary spending.

It puts them in the driver's seat at the start of that uninterrupted theoretical stretch, so that they're able to spend their money more carefully—and, if they get derailed for any reason, to help to keep their eyes on the family's overall, long-term goals, and get back on track. Conversely, for those who don't take the time to analyze how they want to spend their money before embarking on the marathon towards retirement—with interim lifecycle goals along the way—they may end up rudely surprised, 20 years later, to find that much of that $1.5 million in lifetime earnings remains unaccounted for.

Using this Budgeting Guideline formula has now become a real exercise to actively consider and manage our day-to-day spending. From this point of view, we should be able to see the larger and broader impact of consuming versus investing for the long term. Looking from this perspective at what you have to show monetarily from your decisions and actions in your month-to-month cash flow spending is the type of consciousness I want us all to cultivate and keep within us on our financial journey throughout life.

Doing this exercise takes time, energy, and effort. It requires honest reflection and a commitment to change in ways that will probably make most folks uncomfortable. Every time that discomfort sets in and you start thinking about how much "sacrifice" these changes will require, I want you to harken back to our ancestors who fought and died for a better future for the next generation. Think of all those who sacrificed so much, many paying the ultimate price, so that we can explore the wealth of opportunities that we have today. To be blessed with options, choices, and opportunity; the freedom to decide our own journey, and to manifest our own destiny; and to live a higher quality of life are among the legacies that our ancestors left us. Let's put these things into perspective, get and stay on track, and make our whole community stronger!

OPPORTUNITY COST COMPARISONS—PURCHASES VS. INVESTMENTS

Lastly, I want us to talk more in depth about opportunity cost. As previously mentioned, opportunity cost refers to a benefit that a person could have received but gave up because he or she chose to take another, earlier course of action. More technically, in investing, it is the difference in return between a chosen investment and the one that was passed up—not necessarily by choice, but by necessity or due to a lack of adequate resources or knowledge. This is often expressed as the difference between the expected returns of each option.

Opportunity Cost = Return of Most Lucrative Option vs. Return of Chosen Option

When making big decisions like buying a home or starting a business, you will, no doubt, scrupulously research the pros and cons of your financial decision to figure out the best deal, and to see if it makes financial sense. On the contrary, most day-to-day choices are made without full research and consideration of the potential opportunity costs of those decisions. Even when being cautious about a purchase, often the extent of the due diligence performed only involves a review of the bank account balance before spending that money. And it is rare that people think about the things that they must give up when they make those decisions.

We must recognize that this kind of myopic thinking can be dangerous when we fail to look at what else we could do with that money, or when we buy things blindly without considering the lost opportunities. For example, purchasing lunch at work occasionally can be a wise decision if, for instance, it lets you fraternize with your coworkers, cultivate valuable relationships, and glean invaluable "water cooler"-type information in the process. However, buying one cheeseburger every day for the next 25 years could lead to numerous missed opportunities. Aside from the potentially harmful health effects of high cholesterol, taking that $4.50 spent on a burger each day and investing it in the stock market—with a doable, conservative rate of return over 25 years of 5%—could add up to just over $52,000 in that time frame.

Likewise, when we apply this concept to other purchases that we have become accustomed to seeing in our community (e.g., a $2,500 bag, $400 belt, $500 car payment, $350 shoes or sneakers, or a $150 phone bill), we need to be mindful that those same amounts could have generated an even larger return on our initial investment when placed elsewhere, such as a savings vehicle, home purchase, life insurance or annuity, or a capital investment (no matter how small) in an entrepreneurial venture.

A great question to ponder is, "Would you rather have $2,500 in cash in a paper bag, or have a $2,500 luxury bag with no cash in it—and no cash in the bank?" I ask this because these are choices that are made in our community every day with the tragic result being that so many live from paycheck to paycheck because of their unwise decisions. I think a smart guideline and parameter for these types of choices is to make sure that you have 10 times the amount of the desired item in the bank before you make the purchase. That way you are not wearing what should be your financial cushion in the form of a pricy belt or purse.

This brings us to an even deeper conversation on making sure that we also note *what* is steering our purchases and actions. Did a flashy commercial cause you to equate a particular luxury car with wealth and status—and enamor you enough to take out a loan to purchase that vehicle to elevate your own perceived status? Similarly, for what reason are you taking on additional debt, and at what expense? The nice house, nice car, Christmas gifts for thousands of dollars, the latest Jordans, Xbox games, and all the top-shelf items and most coveted gear. Again...at what expense? We can't have 400 pairs of shoes each and nothing in our 401(k)s. We can't spend our entire lives just shopping and accumulating things, so we can "pop tags," as some rap songs brag about. We must realize what the opportunity costs are and what we are sacrificing by over-consuming.

Let's become aware of how we justify, for example, any $350 payment that we make each month. Whether it's going towards a BMW car note, a retirement vehicle, our kids' college savings, or your own student loans. What is the return on that $350 monthly payment—and is it worth it? Let's think about which items in our lives are most important—including our future goals—and prioritize them appropriately. This includes earmarking money in our budget to underwrite those items. A great saying I've heard is: "The wealthy teach their children how to acquire, the rich teach their children how to sell, and the poor teach their children how to buy."

THE WEALTHY TEACH THEIR CHILDREN HOW TO ACQUIRE, THE RICH TEACH THEIR CHILDREN HOW TO SELL, AND THE POOR TEACH THEIR CHILDREN HOW TO BUY.

Let's think about our foundation, accumulation, preservation, and distribution of wealth. Are we accumulating more assets or debt? How does our spending impact our credit report? Let's give greater urgency to sacrificing in the short term, even deferring gratification, and getting our mindset and spending habits in line. As mentioned earlier, for many of us, this means having the intestinal fortitude (read: guts) to do some soul searching about the instrumental role that our own egos, self-esteem issues, insecurities, history, and the myriad emotional and psychological underpinnings have played in our spending habits. Fixing the problem means first *facing* the problem.

Another point to consider is beyond just purchasing an item; there may also be maintenance and upkeep associated with it. We see these issues arise regularly when athletes and entertainers buy houses for which they can't afford to pay the taxes, repairs, utilities, and maintenance services like pool and lawn maintenance later on. I've heard many men say, "I pay my child support." Great. Have you also budgeted to pay for the tutoring needed to make sure your child is getting A's at school, or for extracurricular classes to broaden his or her skillset and exposure? Budgeting should be approached with a holistic, 360° view.

Let's not get caught up in the need for a new car every two years or buying above our means. Another great line I heard is: "The best car to drive is the one that's paid for." Imagine what could be done with that $350–500 payment that was previously allocated for that car note. Another rule is to make sure your car value is at 5% of your house value. In addition, you should not live in an apartment or have a $100,000 house yet drive a $50,000 car. *That's not what the wealthy do.* One more memorable line on this topic—"If you have a landlord *and* a Lexus, then you have a problem."

Lastly, be aware that student loan debt is the fastest-growing debt in the Black community. With the ease and popularity of online classes, which many have enrolled in with the great intention of completing a vocational-trade training program or obtaining a degree, loan debt is skyrocketing. Investing in yourself is worth it if degrees are being completed and applied towards greater income or career opportunities; however, be mindful of the long-term debt that such enrollment can create. Also, before enrolling into any program, make sure that it actually provides the skills, training, licensing, and certification necessary to enter that field. There are a considerable number of people (particularly from Black and Brown communities) who pursued higher learning yet graduated without the accreditation and licensing mandatory to enter their given vocations—and are now stuck with useless degrees *and* student loan debt.

Think for the future, not just the moment. Focus on living below your means—not spending more than you make. Avoid the easy traps. Make sure you're receiving compounded interest in your savings account—not just on your debt payments. Also, acquire foundational assets—such as a home, 401(k), and life insurance—that appreciate and provide tax benefits. Vigorously pursue knowledge opportunities that can expand your earning power—be it college, graduate school, or a vocational certificate. Be mindful of how you spend your money at all levels including packing a sandwich for lunch if you have to. Packing a lunch does not make you a chump; it makes you a champ! Use these spending guidelines to intercept your current patterns to make sure you are doing what it takes to get ahead.

As one more reminder about our history and what makes us a community, this section is about being careful with our financial decisions and about considering consequences. Our ancestors had to be extra mindful of decisions and actions because of the discrimination, violence, and danger that they faced: threats we are still dealing with now. And, just like those who came before us, we must weigh our decisions and their consequences for ourselves, our families, and our community. In some areas of the country, we are becoming a permanent underclass, and some of our neighborhoods are starving to death—literally and figuratively starved of resources, intellectual stimulation, cultural exposure, inspiration, and hope. Our children are dying in the streets, but we can change all of that by doing what is necessary to create a new reality—and thereby securing a new future—for them.

IF WE EVER COME TOGETHER: MILLION-DOLLAR-ME ACTION STEP

As a cash-flow exercise, check your spending:

1. Review and analyze 3 to 6 months of your past spending.
2. Sign up for a service like Mint.com to help lay out and analyze your bank account and credit card spending habits in different formats and views.
3. Meticulously forecast your future spending over the next 3 to 6 months.

It's important to do these steps in the outlined order.

And then finally,

1. Track your actual spending over the next 3 to 6 months, compared with your planned spending.
2. Take time to compare and note whether you are on track with your actual and projected plans. Reconcile with yourself if you are over, and congratulate yourself if you are under. Recalibrate as necessary.
3. Continue this exercise at least once per quarter during the year.

RULE #5.
IT'S NOT WHAT YOU MAKE, IT'S WHAT YOU KEEP

NOW THAT YOU have a financial plan for yourself and a focus around your spending, you will need to compare both of these activities to the plans and best practices favored by the wealthy. I want us to look at the tools and rules that they use for maintaining and maximizing wealth for the long term. The underlying key here is that ***it's not what you make, but what you keep; how long you can keep it for; and what you are able to do with it.*** As we all know, and have seen far too many times, folks make money and blow it in no time, or gain wealth and don't know what to do with the influence that accompanies it. Let's make sure that we don't fall into any of these traps as we increase our wealth.

There are two parts to this discussion:

1. **A clear understanding of the differences between the concepts of income and wealth.** These two concepts can help you to evaluate where you stand financially, but it is the comprehension of wealth that is paramount to our community in closing the wealth gap.

2. **To study and evaluate what those with wealth do with it.** We will see how the affluent build and preserve wealth, use it to influence

and enhance their places in society, and boost their personal legacies.

As a rule, those who've had money longer tend to act *differently* from those with "new" money. We'll explore what that "old money" versus "new money" dichotomy typically looks like—the primary difference is mindset and spending habits. We will then explore some of the typical lifestyle activities that go along with a person's level in life and society, based upon income and wealth status. In this section I will also share some things I believe that we genuinely *don't know that we don't know* and should be focused on, as well as some areas where we are missing opportunities or squandering the ones we were given.

In essence, this chapter is designed to provide you with a greater understanding of *wealth*—specifically *your wealth,* in the context of a bigger economic, historical, political, and social panorama. This enhanced understanding will allow you to better manage your financial plan by relinquishing the idea of keeping up with the Joneses next door, and by embracing the idea of keeping up with the truly wealthy who are managing their money astutely.

PART I
THE DIFFERENCE BETWEEN INCOME AND WEALTH

"Income" and "wealth" have become synonymous in American culture—incorrectly so. While the two concepts often go hand-in-hand, using the terms interchangeably is misleading. America's most wealthy individuals don't necessarily draw the highest levels of income. And many highly paid individuals live from paycheck to paycheck, without any real wealth accumulation.

While professional athletes, top executives, doctors, and lawyers have reputations for high salaries, their obligations can make accumulating significant wealth very difficult. Even positioning oneself to earn a steep salary in a high-profile job or career is generally accompanied by financial commitments—both to get the job in the first place and then to maintain a higher standard of living. Some of the major factors are: paying back student loans, mortgages, home improvements, spending on children, saving for college education, luxury spending, and travel.

In contrast, there are some folks who have never earned a large income but have worked from a young age; paid in-state tuition at a state university; lived well below their means; invested at least 10% of their income; diligently shunned debt; remained in their small three-bedroom homes in their working-class neighborhoods to pay off their mortgages; sent their children to public schools; and bought used cars with cash. While these individuals may not have lived lavish lives, their families are not only comfortable—they're debt free. After 30 years of investing, some who subscribe to this modest way of living have built up investment portfolios worth well over a million dollars.

So, let's clearly define the two: **Wealth** is the net worth of a person—the total value of his or her assets, minus liabilities. Whereas, **income** is the amount of money that a person receives in return for his or her labor, services, sale of goods, or profit from investments. Wealth typically takes a huge amount of time to acquire, as the value of assets and accounts must accrue to increase, while income is earned immediately. We should think of *income* as the amount of money someone receives on a regular basis, such as a biweekly paycheck; and *wealth* as the reservoir of money and assets that can be used for emergencies and opportunities.

Another way you can view these differences is by considering the length of time that a person (or family) could maintain his/her current lifestyle without receiving compensation for performing work. For example, a family that earned $60,000 per year, with over $1 million in investments, could sustain their current lifestyle for more than 16 years without ever needing to work again ($1,000,000/$60,000 = 16 years). The bottom line is that an abundance of wealth creates security and opportunity, and a lack of wealth can create hardship and an inability to harness ways of creating more wealth.

When looking at the Black community, we are behind White America in both income and wealth. Specifically, we can point to the long-standing median household income gap, which, as reported by the Census Bureau in its 2017 "Income and Poverty in the United States" report, showed that, as of 2016, Whites earned $65,041, compared to $39,490 for Blacks. This statistic means that Black households earn 60 cents for every dollar earned by a White household. While we have made gains as a result of increased education (breaking the glass ceiling and so forth), more needs to be done. Wealth is not often discussed in our community, but it represents an even more disparate gap between races. As mentioned before, the average Black family has only 13 cents for every dollar owned by White Americans. So, whether its 60 cents earned or 13 cents owned, Black people are lagging behind their counterparts. This is not only shocking; it is unacceptable.

PART 2
THE WEALTHY AND THEIR MONEY

I was at a meeting a few years ago with former U.S. Ambassador and Atlanta Mayor Andrew Young, and he said, "We've made a lot of people rich in the Black community, but we've not made them wealthy." He was referring to the dearth in our community of long-term, fortune-minded habits that are needed to acquire additional wealth. In this section, I want to talk about what the wealthy do—and don't do—with their money.

I have four children, ages 10 through 16. I'm taken aback by what seems to be their attraction to the glorification of spending millions, carrying suitcases filled with money, rapping about piles and bands of cash, and *braggadociously* spewing out lyrics like, "I have $100,000 on my wrist," based on what they hear on the radio and see on TV and the Internet. These are clearly actions of the newly rich, but they have devastating effects on young, impressionable minds that are bombarded by these enhanced and unrealistic media images. There's a saying: *What they see is what they'll be.* That said, if our children are regularly exposed to the extravagance of athletes and entertainers spending their mon-

> WHAT THEY SEE IS WHAT THEY'LL BE.

ey—largely on depreciating assets—without understanding the need for astute financial planning and responsibility, then we are setting our next generation up for major financial failure.

So what am I telling my children? I feel like I talk to them all the time about these things. But to make sure I'm not just talking to myself, one day I asked my 15-year-old son which of the lessons I've imparted to him that has stood out as valuable. He replied:

> *Be smart with your money, because all of those flashy things in rap songs will go away really quickly. They will not have those things in the next few years, and definitely not in the next 10 to 20 years. Like, you won't have your Jordans or joggers in 20 years. But if you put money into your college fund, then you will have the knowledge and job that will support you in 20 years.*
>
> *You have to set yourself up for the future. It's okay to splurge at times, since we all want nice things, like nice sneakers, but you don't have to spend your entire paycheck or spend all your money. Be balanced with it. If you have money in your bank account and have stuff saved up and you are good for the future, then you can splurge, and buy certain things to treat yourself. But if you don't have a lot of money and you are just spending it on stupid things, then you are always going to be struggling.*

Well OK, I thought. For all the times it appeared that my teenage son wasn't paying attention or was more concerned about his Xbox than my expectations, I was wrong. So much of what I have said to him did sink in, and will hopefully continue to influence his decision-making, going forward.

I am big on saying life is not about living fast and dying young; only being in the moment; chasing fads and fashion; or being a slave to your paycheck and the credit card companies. During my time as a corrections officer, I saw thousands of young Black men in prison who never actually had their own apartments; never owned cars; never experienced life away from their mommies; never participated in mature, loving relationships;

and never traveled the world, or even the rest of the United States. Yet they emulated the materialistic fantasy being projected onto their screens and had become stuck chasing a lifestyle that they'd heard being rapped about and elevated nearly all their lives.

I hope to have a long and fruitful life, like my 96- and 100-year-old Grenadian grandparents, and I am confident that my financial stewardship will ensure that finances are never a concern for my family or me as long as we live. I've already bumped my head more than once, learned from it, and seized the financial reins of my life: There will be no further silly or senseless financial pitfalls for my family that, in the end, gained us nothing, except for a cute picture or post on social media, a thumbs-up emoji, or, worse yet, any of us sitting in a jail cell.

Now I'm going to jump into a discussion on how **Old Money** and **New Money** habits differ. **Old Money** (sometimes referred to as **Family Money**) is the inherited wealth of established upper-class families. The term typically describes a class of the rich who have been able to maintain their wealth over multiple generations. **New Money** or **Nouveau Riche** refers to the man or woman who had previously belonged to a lower social class, but, having recently obtained **New Money**, was able to achieve upward social mobility. This new wealth has provided the means for conspicuous consumption—the buying of goods and services that signal membership in an upper class.

Disclaimer: The descriptions listed in Diagram 18 are not universal, and are not meant to offend, but are merely meant to illustrate a point regarding the trappings that many "new money" folks find themselves in. In sharing this information, I want to make sure that "new money" novices have an opportunity to evolve into "old money" experts. Let's take a look:

Diagram 18.

	Old Money	*New Money*
Investing	Capital preservation, while keeping up with inflation, is their primary objective. They are stewards of their family's wealth for future generations.	They speculate to accumulate. More cavalier, short sighted, and open to risk.
Charitable giving	They see supporting the arts and cultural institutions as an obligation that comes with wealth.	More interested in naming opportunities that reflect back to self than supporting the cultural institution's underlying mission.
Homes	Properties may be large, but not necessarily. Often handed down, or inherited homes family members grew up in. Have no mortgages.	Properties are large, often an over extension to keep up with the Joneses. Used interest-only loans in the mortgage bubble to get bigger homes beyond means.
Home décor	Happy with period furniture and stately antiques. As stated in the television show, *Downton Abbey*, "Your lot buys it, my lot inherits it."	Keep current with trends. Work with interior designers. Invented "fashion furniture," disposing of it every few years.
Cars	Cars are transportation. They aren't meant to attract attention. "Maintain something well, and it will last forever."	Your car is your rolling net-worth statement. "You are what you drive."
Clothing	Own well-made clothing, maintained over time. Designer items are often years old. Quality comes first.	Stylish. Lots of *new,* current-season designer-label items. Can only wear something once, publicly.

	Old Money	*New Money*
Travel	Are well traveled, but don't announce it directly. When talking amongst themselves, they know details of streets in major cities, and the must-see current theater productions—from New York's Broadway to London's West End.	It's not only where you went, but also how much you spent, the name of the hotel, and size of the suite.
The second home	Have summer houses at the shore or in the mountains. Working spouse stays in the city weekdays and returns to second home on weekends.	Where you summer is important. Rent a house in the Hamptons or on the Vineyard. Let everyone know—and invite people to visit.
Spending habits	Surprisingly, wealthy people often come across as cheap. They like getting a good deal, but don't talk about it. They never talk about how much they've paid—and might actually complain about high prices. Openly bragging about how much they have paid is seen as lowbrow and vulgar.	Get the biggest and most expensive of whatever they're buying to make a statement. *Splurge* is a favorite verb.
Talking about wealth	Very strategic and methodical in passing investment advice on to the next generation, while the family is seated at the dinner table.	They talk about spending constantly.
Hire help	May have a nanny or housekeeper, but most don't hire full-time staff. Cook meals and serve guests themselves. Many clean their own homes, too.	The hiring of staff is a conspicuous display of wealth. They don't clean their own home. Complain about the difficulty of finding good help.

	Old Money	*New Money*
Eat in or eat out?	Do eat out, but largely like to entertain at home. Do their own cooking. Meals can be simple. Chili is fine. However, enjoy throwing formal receptions as well. Own all the entertaining accouterments, which were often wedding presents.	Primarily entertain by dining out. Couples split the check down the middle. The grander the kitchen, the less likely it's ever used.

Some of these comparative descriptions are overly broad—even comical—but among them are many grains of truth about the differences between Old Money and New Money. More important, the long-term intention is for New Money to transition into Old Money. This, for the most part, will happen over generations, as long as wealth is maintained. However, these illustrations depict the proclivity and priority of the newly rich to spend so that they can brag, which may not allow their money to last for the long term—much less more intergenerationally. My hope is that you will consider the differing mindsets and habits for yourself, align with the status and expectations of moving into new circles, and be mindful of how your decisions will maintain your wealth. The next section will explore the activities that new wealth and social status afford.

THE "LIFESTYLE ACTIVITIES CHART"

I received the "Lifestyle Activities" chart in Diagram 19 at an executive-training program several years ago. Upon reviewing it, I wondered why I had never seen it before, and why it is not distributed on a larger scale. Perhaps it is because it can be seen as very stereotypical, and it clearly isn't representative of all people and all families in our community. But, since other folks are looking at it, I want us all to look at it, too. The intention of this book is to share the untold tools and rules and to make sure that we're included in the conversations others around us are having.

Diagram 19: Lifestyle Activities.
Source: Executive Leadership Council

Categories	*One*	*Two*	*Three*
Socio-economic Class Titles	Dropout Class	Lower Class, Welfare, Poverty	Lower-Middle Class, Working Class, Blue Collar
Education	1–2 Years of High School	Possibly High School Degree	Usually High School Degree
Occupation	Out of Work	Part-time Worker at Minimum Wage	Non-exempt, Manual, Administrative Workers
Organizations and Clubs	Church Club	YMCA/YWCA, Boys/Girls Clubs, Church Clubs	Cultural Clubs, Gun Clubs, Lodges
Social Activities	Church Related	TV, Church	Movies, Hunting, Fishing, Camping, Family Activities, Bowling
Location and Type of House	Urban, Homeless, Housing Projects	Urban, Housing Projects, Rent Subsidized	Urban Areas, Own Mobile Homes
Entertaining in the Home	Rarely Entertain	Extended Family Members, Holidays	Family and Friends, Barbeques, Casual
Earning Power	None	$8,000–$15,000	$12,000–$60,000
Other Investments	None	None	Savings, Series "E" Bonds, Lottery Tickets
Fine Arts	Never Attended Theater	Rarely Attends Theater	Attends Popular Theater Productions
Car	No Car	1 Used Car	Intermediate Used Car, Pickup Truck
Vacations	None	Home to Parents	1-Week Family Vacation, Home to Parents
Committees and Boards	Not Involved	Involved in Church Work	Nonprofit, Community Volunteer Work

Diagram 19: Lifestyle Activities (cont'd).
Source: Executive Leadership Council

Four	Five	Six	Seven
Middle Class, White Collar, Managerial, Professional	Upper Middle Class, High Level	Lower Upper Class, Celebrity, Nouveau Riche, Jet Set	Upper Class, Governing Elite, Aristocratic, Old Money,
Technical and Associate Degree	College Degree, Solid Schools	Advanced Degree, Better Schools	Advanced Degree, Best Schools, Boarding/Prep
Exempt, Accountants, Programmers, Sales Reps, Managers	Middle Management, Small Business Owners, Medical Professionals	Regional/State Politicians, Corporate Execs, Movie/ TV/Sports Personalities	Family Business, National Politics, Wall Street Attorneys, Top-20 Banks
Mason, Rotary, Nonprofit, Civic Organizations	Neighborhood Country Clubs, Swim/Tennis Clubs	Regional Country Clubs, Local Community Boards	Exclusive National Social Clubs, Nonprofit and Corporate Boards
Entry Level, Theater, Tennis, Golf	More Accomplished in Sports and Cultural Events	Sailing, Skiing, Flying, Charity Drives	Yachting, Horse Breeding, Fox Hunting, Polo, Fine-Arts Patron
Suburban Communities, Own Tract Homes	Country-Club Communities, In-town Renovations	Extra-Large Homes, Custom Built, Tennis Court, Pool	Mansions, Multiple Homes
Social Cocktail Parties, Self- Prepared, Sporty	Cocktail Parties, Business and Social, Catered, Dressy	Dinner Parties Business and Social, Catered, Dressy	Dinner Parties, Very Political, Extravagant, Formal
$18,000–$125,000	$100,000–$300,000	$250,000-Billions	$100s of Millions, Inherited Wealth
Urban Condo, IRAs, CDs, Treasury Bonds	Vacation Home, Investment Portfolio	Limited/General Partnership, Revenue Properties	Stock Ownership, Interlocking Directories
Theater, Ballet, Opera, Symphony, Museum	Season Tickets Ballet, Opera, Symphony, Museum	Serve on Fine-Arts Committees and Boards	Fine-Arts Patron
Big American Cars, 1 Other Used Car	Mercedes, Cadillac, Other Luxury Cars	Rolls Royce, Bentley, Multiple Cars	Chauffeur-Driven Limousine
1-Week Shore, Mountains, 1-Week Home to Parents	USA Vacation, Cruises, Shore, Mountains	Exclusive Resorts, Abroad Once a Year	Most Exclusive Resorts, Extended Vacation Abroad, Seasonal Home
On Committees of Nonprofit Organizations	Chair Committees of Major Nonprofit Organizations	On Boards of Nonprofit, Regional Corporations, Local Arts	Chair Boards of National Corporations/Nonprofits, Fine Arts Organizations

This chart provided me with a new perspective on things to consider for my life, based upon my current income and financial success, and the corresponding social status that my increasing income levels afford me in society. I am sharing it here as a window into the various investments, focuses, and activities for the range of socioeconomic levels in America. Many of us may not be privy to these lifestyles if we don't know anyone at any level other than our own and haven't had an opportunity to peer into what the top 10% and 1% of wage earners are doing.

I have reviewed this chart many times over the years, and I want to share some of those insights with you. First, this chart clearly reinforces what we are told as children: Education (formal or vocational) will lead to your occupation, and that will lead to your income. From there goes your path in life—ranging from the size and location of your home, to your investments, to the kinds of activities you have access to.

Having worked in a maximum-security prison for four years, I'd like to take this point further. The first column highlights for me the likely predetermined destiny of a lot of our young men in the Black community that are on the path to dropping out of school. As the chart shows, they are likely setting themselves up as soon as they start to distance themselves from schoolwork, act out in class, get bad grades, and fall behind. I know that I felt the peer pressure to look cool as a teenager in Brooklyn, and my subsequent focus on girls also took a great deal of my attention.

However, it should be acknowledged that a lot of young people (as well as adults) in our community have experienced a tremendous amount of unresolved trauma (ranging from physical and sexual abuse, to having witnessed, or been the victims of, violent crimes) that contribute to this acting out or a lack of focus. This often leads to truancy issues or academic underperformance—which can mark the start of a vicious cycle that ends in enough of our young people dropping out of school to continue to cause concern. If you glance down the rows of the "Drop-out Class" column in Diagram 19, the opportunities are slim. If you start to overlay the likely court system and subsequent jail and prison impact, then the cycle of not getting ahead continues for this group—often for life.

As we continue to move across the top of the chart, we can start to see that some individuals might view basic investments as things like lottery tickets, whereas owning and operating small businesses might be the focus for others. We can start to see how one's world view and perspective might change from broadened activities and exposure, as seen moving horizontally across the chart. Whereas some in our community primarily talk about things like sports, sneakers, and parties, with cultural exposure, they can begin to talk about things like vacations, theater, and becoming involved in political causes, and cultural and charity events.

I want to make it clear that I'm not being elitist. Such cultural activities and enrichment don't always require a lot of money, or sometimes any money, from participants. Programs and institutions like the Boys & Girls Clubs of America, public libraries, civic organizations, and nonprofits provide discounts or free programming for low-income culture seekers. However, that's the point—they have to *want* to seek the arts, special programs, and such horizon-widening opportunities. In addition, volunteering for community and political organizations requires no money—just commitment. While it should be done with a heart to serve, such volunteering can also lead to a widened social circle that includes people from across the socioeconomic spectrum, as well as additional opportunities—some of them *paid.*

The chart also made me think of how skewed some of our reality-television shows are that highlight "housewives," "hip-hop," and "cribs," with a clear emphasis on spending and accumulating name-brand products and living lavish lifestyles. What we don't see as often are the corresponding higher-culture activities and philanthropic endeavors that accompany a more responsible, nuanced, and civic-minded approach to wealth. Regardless of our financial level, we can all become philanthropically-minded by providing for hurricane victims, or enhancing contributions to our local schools, and creating safety zones for children in urban areas. These could provide amazing, inspiring visuals to social media—fueled, not by celebrity giving, but by *our* giving to, and taking care of, those in our own communities, as well as others in need.

Another point to consider is making sure that our children are provided with the best support structures to ensure their success—beyond parental love, affection, and guidance. Acquire academic tutors to keep them on task, expose them to extracurricular activities beyond traditional sports (skiing, tennis, sailing, music, art, debate, etc.), enroll them in test preparation courses, and instill in them a philanthropic spirit by requiring that they participate in community-service activities. Doing so will equip them with the ability to adapt to an ever-changing world, to present themselves as well-rounded, cultured individuals, and to prepare them to take advantage of any and all opportunities that may arise. Regardless of the economic level at which they *start*, this is how our children will move across the top of the chart as they grow into their own lives and are clear on some of the other things that they'll need to build an upward path in life.

I also want to share how this chart can be used as an aspirational guide. I'm thinking specifically of those who are looking for a partner, spouse, or life mate, as they plan the financial roadmaps for their life journey. They can now look at things to talk about, and to plan to achieve, together. It's not solely about making six figures and driving a BMW, but the full complement of a couple living, building, sustaining, and being on the same page about where they are going in life—as a unit. Such agreement and union by a couple on what they want to achieve and the sacrifices they're willing to make to get there provides a North Star for life.

While some of you might still be offended by what is listed on this chart, again, I don't present it to cast judgment. I would implore you to see it as articulating general guidance regarding the types of things that we should be considering for our own lives. It's not meant to be held up as *the* benchmark. It only provides perspective, letting you know where you are and what can and can't be reconciled for you to grow and move forward.

For example, if you fall into the "Five" category for the row titled "Car," and you rank a "Two" in all the other rows, then that should sound an alarm bell for you to pause and reflect. (Here's an example: driving a Bentley but living in the hood...and filling it up with the lowest grade of gas, at a run-down, no-name gas station—yes, I have seen it with my own eyes.) In that way, the chart provides context: We may think that we're fine where we are, and our family and friends may think the same thing of us and of themselves. Alternatively, we may think we're fine because the kinds of experiences that we've had to date are *all* we know. Hopefully this chart shows what *else* is out there in the world for you to consider adding to your life—be it easily obtainable, or aspirational. The context that the chart provides also helps us to understand how others with money are managing their lives differently in a number of areas.

I have looked upon the chart many times and realized that I've fallen in between categories, meaning that I have been doing one thing and getting ahead, but had been derelict in, or not been paying attention to, other areas. It has, therefore, made me more cognizant of my need for community and board service, my desire to actually visit a museum or gallery more regularly to understand fine arts, and to take another golf lesson. My goal is to continue to evolve into a more cultured and well-rounded individual, with a dynamic life full of multiple components and contributions.

Even the renewal of my subscriptions to *Savoy* and *Black Enterprise* magazines, and my watching the Sunday shows *Our World with Black Enterprise* with Marc Lamont Hill and *Here and Now* with Sandra Bookman, were spurred on by reflecting on this chart.

This chart also helped me to put my financial goals and spending habits into perspective: for example, deciding to keep a modest, older car, but planning more extravagant overseas vacations. And I've thought about other ways to regulate what I've been doing as my career continues to progress, my investments grow, and my activities have matured. I have discussed it all with my fiancée as we dream and plan our future, and that of our blended family, to make sure that we are balanced with these areas as models for our children. We also discuss these concepts with our children. The chart has truly helped to answer some of my own questions, such as: "Have I arrived, and—if not—what's next for me to achieve in my American dream?"

I'll end this section and discussion by complimenting some in our community who have created some new **rules** and smarter concepts for members of our community to model themselves after, in terms of focus and actions: Jay-Z, Beyoncé, LeBron, Rihanna, and Diddy have now evolved their lavish spending into investments that allow them to capture and profit from the spending of others. And they've made civic and philanthropic investments in high-impact areas such as education. They now say things to the effect of: *Don't buy the bottle, buy the bar; don't buy the clothes, start a fashion line; don't just buy the car, buy the dealership; and don't just give me an endorsement, give me part of the company*. This is powerful.

In addition, more recent celebrities like Chance the Rapper have become outstanding role models for community giving. Check out *New Visions in Business Magazine* (now online), which regularly showcases individuals like him.

This leads me to say that we must also be forward thinking, and participate in the industrial shift to technology, to build next-generation wealth. Let's not just use the app but create one. Let's not just use the platform, or even simply buy the stock, but create our own tech firms. Let's not just hear the words coding and artificial intelligence ("AI"); let's push our children to participate in, and perhaps dominate, this new space.

THE UPCOMING MASS TRANSFER OF WEALTH, AND OUR PLACE IN IT

Now that you know some of the rules and have heard how others are playing the wealth game, I want to put into context something huge that is happening around us: There is a growing focus on the greatest-*ever* transfer of wealth that will happen over the next 20 years, due to Baby Boomers' retirements and the subsequent passing on of their assets. The staggering number being estimated in this transfer is around $20 trillion. As a result of this anticipated influx and movement in money, there is a widespread focus, by financial companies, accountants, and lawyers offering and adapting products and planning to maximize returns, as well as politicians who are setting up laws to support the shift, with tax advantages for the wealthy.

I want to make sure that we participate in this wealth transfer, so I'm pulling back the curtains and making sure that you know that it's happening. Because of this transfer, the sections we just explored in this chapter will be ever-more important to keep in mind. Remember, you can't earn your way to wealth. You need assets and investments growing for the long term for yourself, and to pass on to future generations. This massive wealth transfer will cause us to fall even further behind if we don't become even *more* proactive about closing the wealth gap now!

As Rule #5, the title of this chapter says, "It's Not What You Make, It's What You Keep." The current $571,000 wealth gap for the average Black family is projected to balloon to $1 million by 2043. As I mentioned, we're also dealing with the challenge of the 41.7% home-ownership rate in our community, versus 72.2% for White America—and how to create parity in those numbers. Billions of dollars in wealth are being transferred every year via policies underwritten by major life insurance companies. Now, that steady stream will become a geyser, as families from other communities around us will move $20 trillion from one generation to the next over the next 20 years.

In the atmosphere of this unprecedented wealth transfer, let's stay laser focused on how we're going to catch up, keep up, and get ahead as a community. Let's start here: *Live below our means, limit the symbols of wealth, curb excessive spending, create an inheritance plan, and expand our conversations about wealth at the barbeque like they do at the country club.* And let's continue to read more broadly and learn even more, as well as connect and rub elbows with those who have already arrived at where we aspire to go—even if we can only rub *virtual* elbows with them on social media!

IF WE EVER COME TOGETHER: MILLION-DOLLAR-ME ACTION STEP

Assess your wealth and your health. Are all areas of your life proliferating wealth? Are you as wealthy, from a health and wellness standpoint, as you are monetarily, or do you suffer from chronic illness, pain, or fatigue? Likewise, do you have a wealth of education? Are you reading books, taking classes, and always learning and getting better?

How are you *enriching* all the other areas of your life?

Please take time to make your own assessments about where you are and where you want to be.

RULE #6. RICH PEOPLE PLAN FOR THREE GENERATIONS, AND POOR PEOPLE PLAN FOR SATURDAY NIGHT

NOW THAT WE'VE looked at ourselves individually on the path to wealth, I want to share some tools and rules I've learned for expanding and ensuring wealth for our families, as well as for our businesses, institutions, and the causes we care about. These strategies encompass both estate and legacy planning for you, your direct family, and your community. Many of us either don't know, or have not been focused on, these powerful insights. We will examine the application of so-called *Advanced-Planning* concepts to have collective financial impact on your families, businesses, and cherished institutions and organizations.

Specifically, we are going to detail ideas for: planning across at least three generations in a family; protecting through wills and trusts; properly passing on property in neighborhoods undergoing gentrification; fortifying your family businesses; and conducting succession and transition planning up to two or three generations ahead.

This chapter is about supporting one another and the collective leveraging of tools and strategies to build wealth across the Black community. A great framework for this discussion comes from former First Lady

WE'VE GOT A RESPONSIBILITY TO LIVE UP TO THE LEGACY OF THOSE WHO CAME BEFORE US BY DOING ALL THAT WE CAN TO HELP THOSE WHO COME AFTER US.

Michelle Obama, who said: " We've got a responsibility to live up to the legacy of those who came before us by doing all that we can to help those who come after us." Our wealth strategies must transcend tangible consumer items and immediate gratification that don't empower generations to come, or honor the sacrifices of our ancestors. It's time to focus on measures to combat the wealth gap with intentionality, utilizing family inheritance, property transfer, small-businesses succession, and organizational strength.

FAMILY PLANNING

For this chapter, let's be strategic about creating intergenerational wealth to cover at least three generations. The agents and financial advisors at my company have taught me some interesting strategies that they have gleaned from other cultures to achieve this goal. I am fortunate to have both my parents and my children close to me, and we have been able to work together to ensure that the financial future of the Mitchell family will be very positive through an established plan to transfer significant wealth inheritance for generations to come. It is not that we have millions today, but that we are leveraging financial tools to make that happen over generations. I'm not sharing this accomplishment to brag, but to merely show that you can do it, too.

Dr. George Fraser, CEO of FraserNet, reinforced this concept with this powerful quote: "Rich people plan for three generations, and poor people plan for Saturday night." Let's take a look at what we've done, along with ensuring that the appropriate financial-planning documents—like wills and trusts—are in place to solidify the future of where and how we want that transferred wealth to go.

First Generation—Parents: After learning several years ago how other cultures in my Brooklyn neighborhood were pooling resources to place life insurance policies on their parents, as shrewd financial investments and a means of creating their own inheritance, my sister and I approached our parents about doing the same. As you can imagine, they were *extremely* resistant at first. Eventually, they warmed to the idea after several conversations and the reassurance that we were not trying to profit off their deaths or (one must laugh) cause their early demise. My sister and I promised that we would use the money generated from the policies to pay for their grandchildren's and great-grandchildren's college educations, and as down payments for their future home purchases. When the grandchildren receive this inheritance, we will be able to say: It is a *legacy gift* to you from your grandparents, as they intended to lead by example as the matriarch and patriarch of a new future for our family.

The positioning of this conversation as *legacy creation* is how we overcame the emotional and cultural hang-ups that my parents had around the conversation about death, and, particularly, about life insurance. Once they grasped the concept, they said: "You can insure us, but we are not going to pay for it. You will have to pay the premiums yourself and create your own inheritance." They added, "Now we can focus more on ourselves, and maybe even sell the house and investment we've accumulated to have a blast spending it all."

After laughing at their jokes, we moved on to the serious business of consulting our agent. We agreed that we would purchase a $500,000 universal life insurance policy that covered both parents. This meant that both would have to pass away before my sister and I received the insurance proceeds. By structuring the single policy with two people insured before payout, especially with my mother being 10 years younger than my dad, it made the payments significantly less expensive than if we had structured the policies individually.

Using a joint policy as a way to lower cost, or to insure someone with less-than-perfect health, is one of the first *Advanced-Planning* concepts I want to communicate in this chapter. By structuring the policy this way, my sister and I paid a premium of $300 a month, splitting the payments into $150 each. It is a permanent policy that will never expire, and it builds cash value and receives interest and dividends. The actual cash value amount has grown handsomely over the last ten years, and my sister and I were able to borrow against it when we needed immediate cash.

I want to note that when I've spoken to people about this purchase during some of the corporate seminars I've conducted, I've queried them: "What else in America can you spend $150 on that yields a *guaranteed, tax-free* half-million dollars at some point in the future?" This financial strategy simply shows the power of life insurance as the life-enhancing investment tool it was created to be, able to change a family's dynamics and its future financial trajectory. I think about how many could and should be doing this in the Black community, and the impact this level of basic generational planning can have. The cost for my sister and me is the same as for a cell phone or cable bill. While we were fortunate to receive this information—thanks to my line of business—it shocks and pains us that so many in our community are unaware that they can do this. If you didn't before, now *you know what you didn't know.*

Second Generation—Self: As you will recall in Rule #2, I shared how I discovered my personal financial replacement value to be worth at least $2.5 million by using the calculation shared with me at my job (my earnings at the time of $100,000 per year X the 25 years I would continue to work until my retirement). As a loving spouse and father, I should have $2.5 million worth of life insurance to ensure that, whether I lived that long or passed before that, my family would receive that future income from me.

I purchased mostly term insurance at first, with only a few hundred thousand as permanent life insurance coverage, as that was the most cost-efficient manner of doing so, considering that my children were young. Moreover, I anticipated my salary increasing over time, and that I would be able to pay off other debts to free up cash flow in the future. As planned, I have since begun to convert some of those term policies, as well as renew my 5- and 10-year policies as they expired over time. I have also borrowed against cash value, replaced it, and borrowed again. Remember that, earlier in the book, I spoke of using such policies as our own bank, with a semi-compulsory savings component. Make sure that you and your loved ones don't miss out on these sorts of opportunities.

I want to note that I started with a $100,000 whole life policy when I was 25 years old, acting upon the recommendation of an old friend who was a lot more financially shrewd than I was back then. It cost me $77 a month. I still have it and borrowed against it often in my younger days. The payment always automatically came out of my checking account, and I was wise enough to keep it going. Over the years, as I've appreciated my value and grown my family, I've also added more term coverage, which has been rather inexpensive to do. At one point, I dropped an additional $100,000 whole life policy that I had purchased prior to my marriage but couldn't afford when finances got tight during my divorce. Looking back, 10 years later, I regret having done so, as it's a lot more expensive to restart that $100,000 policy now than it would have been to have kept it going.

While I was still in the corporate world, I also purposely redirected retirement savings dollars that didn't receive my company's 401(k) match (3% at the time) into paying for my life insurance protection instead. This switch in funneling investment dollars is one way that I budgeted for the policies for my children, my parents, and me (I also own property and have investments in my 401(k) allocation, so my foundational assets are diversified).

What I also changed over time in my budget—to ensure that I can always afford life insurance, which is a top priority—was trading in my BMW X5 for a three-year-old Honda Accord EXL. The latter is a more economical commuter vehicle, since I'm on the road so frequently back and forth between the city and the suburbs visiting my children; plus, I realized that the maintenance and upkeep is a fraction of the cost. For instance, it's $60 to replace a Honda tire, versus $350 for a BMW SUV one. Another example: Gas during the recession was $40/tank for regular in the Honda, compared to $100/tank for the premium grade required for the BMW.

Other—very deliberate—changes that I have made in my personal life include things like more date nights at home, bonding over a jointly prepared home-cooked meal and a bottle of wine, and weekend getaways that are within driving distance, instead of needing to fly. We also use the points that we've accrued on our credit cards from former flights when we've traveled to cover the cost of hotels and meals for future trips.

Here are some inexpensive activities we've also opted for—in lieu of higher-priced ones—to spend quality time with our children: riding bikes on the weekends; using a $5 pay-per-view movie service and microwave popcorn, instead of paying $15 per ticket for a family of six, accompanied by ridiculously overpriced movie theater snacks; and cancelling our subscription to premium television channels and DVRs in favor of catching shows the next time they air or on the app.

In addition, I rarely spend time at the mall researching and acquiring the latest fashions. The reality is that I—like so many others out there—have a closet full of clothes that I rarely wear or that still have the tags on them. Whenever I start thinking that it's time to go shopping, I opt first to go into my own closet to see if I really need something new. Like my father would do, I buy a bottle of vodka for $30 and socialize at home with good friends, instead of paying $18 for a single martini (not including tip) at a bar in New York City. Employing some of these strategies can hopefully help you find a few hundred dollars a month for yourself and your family that can be used to pay for a life insurance policy that—at the end of the day—will garner you and your family substantially more benefits in the long run.

Third Generation—Children: After learning that people of other cultures were insuring their parents, I learned that some people placed life insurance policies on their children as another shrewd investment tool and long-term wealth-building strategy. The more I researched it, the more I realized the many benefits of starting early. Policies on children are relatively less expensive, because the child is younger and usually healthier and there is a lesser probability of payout for many years to come.

Hence, the cash value builds up over a longer time span (perhaps 50+ years), so the cash value side of the investment is very attractive on a permanent policy. Additional benefits include locking in insurability, so that the child will always have a policy in place, regardless of how his or her health changes in the future. For families that have genetic and hereditary issues, taking advantage of this should be a no brainer. Another great point is that life insurance and the cash-value buildup is excluded from the Free Application for Federal Student Aid (FAFSA). My intention is to ultimately pass these policies directly on to my children, with the cash value exceeding the policy face amount, based on how they are structured.

Let me get specific to show what I mean by that: I purchased a whole life policy on my daughter when she was a year old, with a predetermined time frame of payment to be only 20 years (meaning that it will be paid in full at that time, and in effect for her entire life). The policy costs me $143 per month, and it is for $250,000 in face-amount coverage. From the expected buildup of the guaranteed cash value in this policy, and assuming that the current dividend scale continues to be invested back into the policy by the company, I can expect to have the following:

- $35,000 saved in the policy that we will have access to by the time she is ready for college, or
- $66,000 in time for her wedding at 25, or
- $124,000 for a house down payment when she is 35, or
- $750,000 toward her retirement at age 65.

Each of these scenarios is possible, depending on whether we choose to use the option to take out the money. This idea of gifting is what we talked about as family financial support—and one of the major contributors of the racial wealth gap. As Black folks, we typically don't have this kind of money to give to our children or other family members. From this illustration, you can see the benefits to both my daughter and me while we are alive, and she will always have that insurance policy in-force when she passes away. Over the duration of the policy, it can benefit her children and her future family. I think of having this policy in place as an estate that I am helping to create for my daughter, and, as I once heard someone say, the "wings of financial freedom" that I can pass on to her as part of my legacy.

As I share this concept of insuring my own child, I know that there are great emotional and cultural hang-ups around life insurance on children. Conversations on the topic have been touchy, with people being sensitive about even considering insuring a child beyond the basic Gerber policies we see advertised on the television or in the hospital packets when a child is born. I'd just like to ask that you step back and take the emotion out of the equation to see that this is one way that others are ensuring that their children get ahead, understanding that many of us are falling behind because we are not open to even hearing this concept.

Best-case scenario: The insured child reaps the benefits listed above. Worst-case scenario (God forbid): The child dies as a youth or young adult. The silver lining in this bleak outcome, however, is that the policy will pay enough—well beyond the funeral expenses—for the parent(s) to have the means and flexibility to take time off to grieve. If I ever found myself in such a devastating situation, I couldn't imagine what I would do if had to rush back to work to sustain myself financially. In addition, the proceeds of a $250,000 policy could be used to establish a memorial or scholarship in the child's memory, providing much needed solace at a time of such loss.

Now that I've shown how you can put plans in place for three generations, you can use the *Financial Family Tree* that follows to discuss the concept with multiple generations in your family.

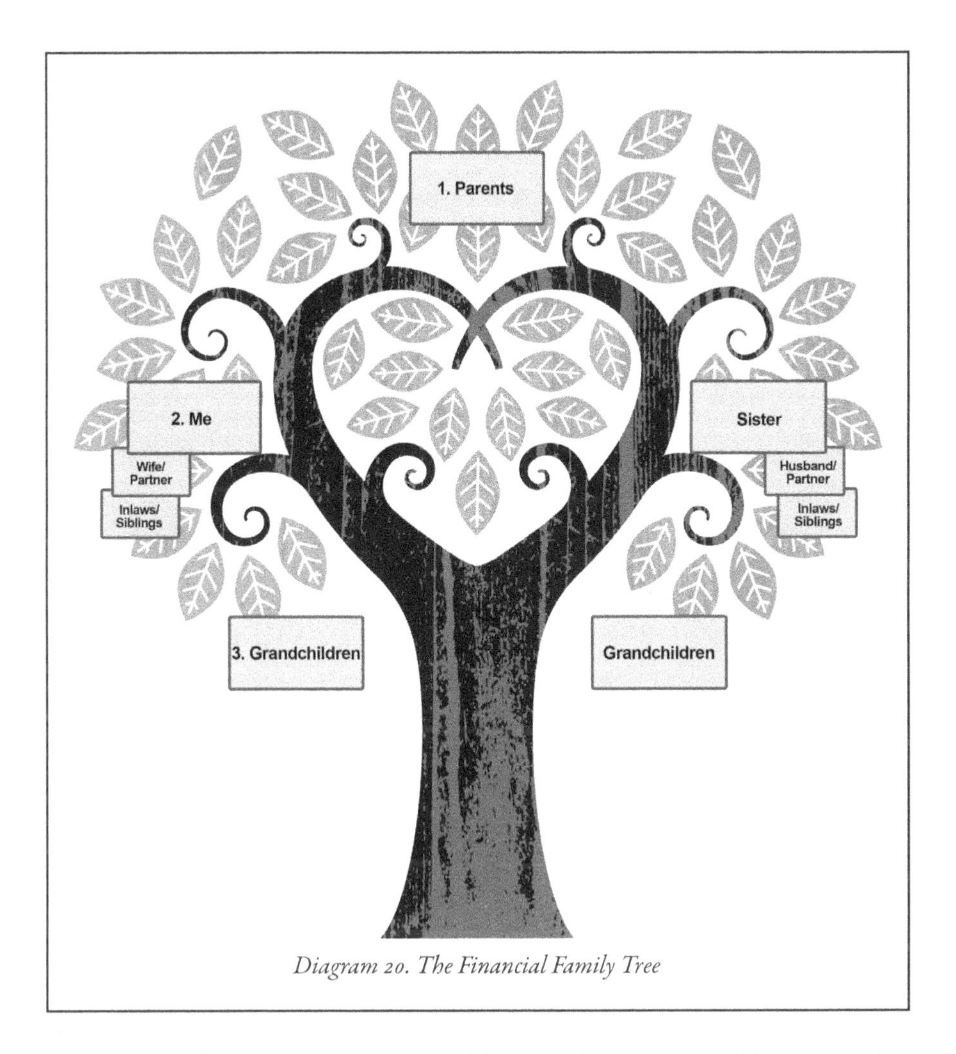

Diagram 20. The Financial Family Tree

The center of the leaves is typically blank so that you can fill it out in the manner that best fits your particular family dynamic. For my family structure, I want to cover three generations. I put my parents in the center, and then included my children and myself down the left side, and my sister and her children down the right side. My intention in laying out the family this way is that it shows the legacy being created by my parents to frame our discussions on intergenerational wealth creation.

Notice that, next to our direct family line in the diagram, there is space for spouse, significant other, life partner, siblings, etc., so that we can continue to share the vision and build the family tree together with everyone in our lives included. Placing the extended family on the side branches also fulfills my parents' intention of focusing their interests on their own two children and grandchildren. As they would say, their Mitchell bloodline should be taken care of, and our marriages and blended families along the way should not dilute or reduce the gifts intended for their direct heirs. This is a personal choice among each family and a totally understandable intention on my parents' part, particularly considering the many horror stories of great intentions gone awry within families, as spouses and stepchildren, as well as aunts and uncles, started laying claim to inheritances and assuming leadership positions to control interests and outcomes.

As a potential antidote to this dynamic, I will also share a little about establishing a will and trust to ensure that the wishes of the head(s) of the family are realized.

In Diagram 21, you will see that I inserted the respective life insurance policy amounts we previously discussed for each of the three generations. I'll illustrate how, through these life insurance policies alone, my family can achieve a multimillion-dollar intergenerational empire. Adding $500,000 (my parents' insurance) + $2,500,000 (mine) + $250,000 (for each of my two children—$250,000 X 2) = $3,500,000 is to be realized. And beyond that life insurance, we could include all of the other transferable assets for wealth building we own, like property, investments, businesses, and so forth.

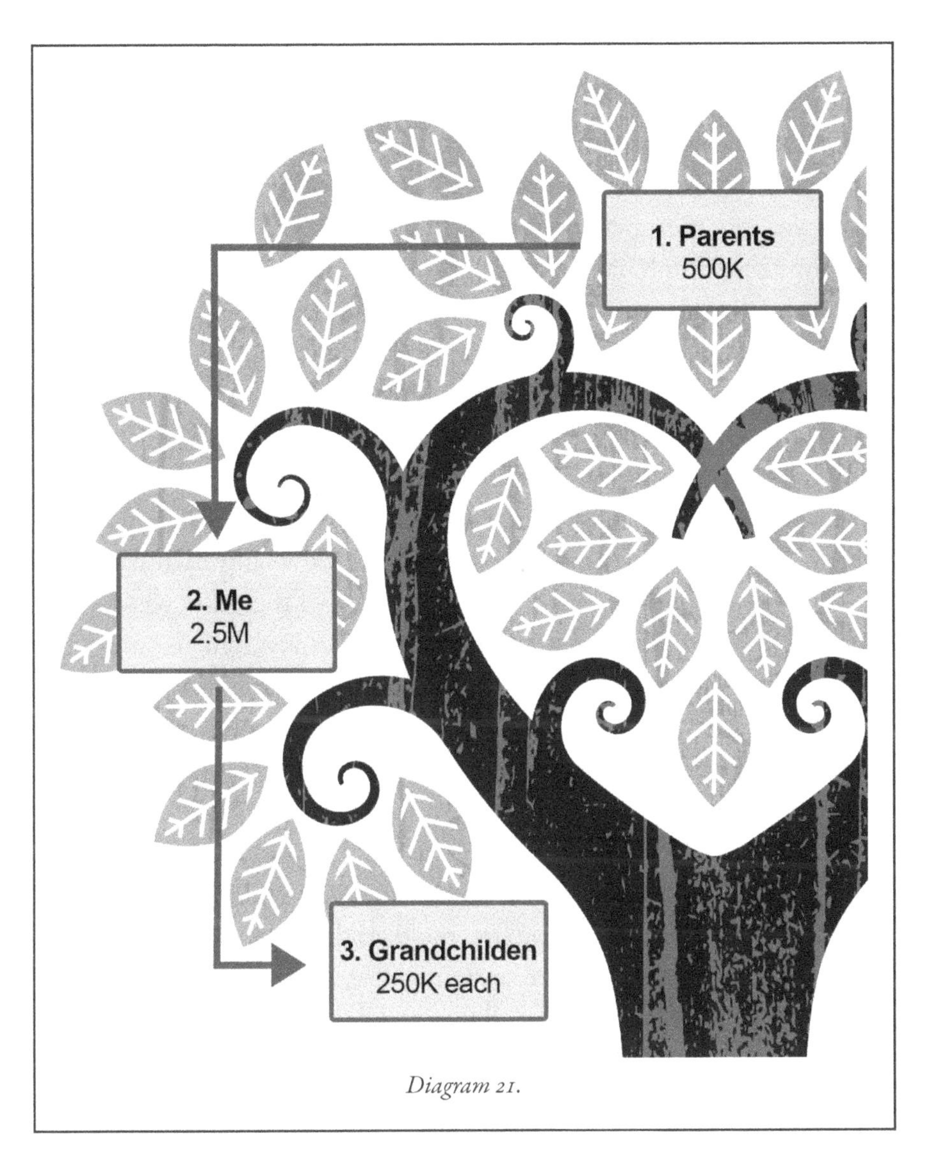

Diagram 21.

As I have sat and thought about these policies over the years, I felt great pride and satisfaction at what our family is creating for my children. While human life is priceless, having these *Financial Family Tree* conversations with my children has allowed me to tangibly show how I value them and their worth. These exchanges also give me an opportunity to express my higher expectations for my kids, because they need to "live up to" the support and legacy the two prior generations have provided for them.

Another point to note is how my significant other and I have both purchased life insurance policies to cover each other's respective ownership stake and mortgage obligation in the home we purchased jointly. Even though we both had coverage on ourselves to benefit our children as part of the divorce stipulations and settlements from our respective former marriages, now, our future planning for our blended family unit incorporates the monetary cost associated with the unfortunate possibility of my fiancée or me not being present for our family.

What started off as my fiancée and me each carrying half of the joint mortgage evolved into additional life insurance coverage to directly benefit the other. This is because we know how we would each be affected—not only emotionally, but also financially—if the other passed. The degree of that impact would be far greater than just half the mortgage amount. So, I want to make sure that my fiancée's life is not materially disrupted, financially or otherwise, in the event of my untimely death. This is another one of those things to think about for all of the people you truly love.

As I have stated repeatedly, wealth provides opportunity and options. Now, with this chart illustrating our accumulating family wealth, I can see an even stronger need to advise, mold, and monitor my children regarding their opportunities and options in life. This is so that they can be money-wise and appreciative of all that will be afforded to them—rather than spoiled or arrogant in their mindsets and actions. If we impart this knowledge about their worth to our children from the time that they are infants, reminding them that they are going to be millionaires in their own right from what they will earn for themselves (earnings over 40+ years) and what they will inherit from the family upon our deaths ($3+ million), then they should have a greater confidence and clarity about themselves and their future.

Another foundational teaching that would flow from this knowledge is that our children should not jeopardize all that they have in front of them by engaging in risky behavior or foolishness that could lead to incarceration, violence, or bad relationships where they are not being treated properly. If they are indeed *Million-Dollar Assets,* then they should act accordingly and expect their spouses, friends, and bosses to treat them as such. Growing up with this sense of value, underpinned by the actual financial foundation to go with it, they should be able to enjoy similar privileges that we know others around us have. Empowering them financially also serves to empower them in every other aspect of their lives. No part of this mindset I'm describing is tied to material possessions or misguided personal value.

I am reminded of a conversation that I once had at the rehearsal for the wedding of a good business school friend of mine. We talked about our expectations for our children. I explained to the groom that the five friends in our circle—me, him, the best man, and the two other groomsmen—were all now working similar corporate jobs and making around the same salary.

I dove into my usual speech about being worth $2.5 million each, but this time I highlighted that, collectively, our insurance for that amount, coupled with our future earnings, would create $12.5 million in inheritance for our children one day ($2,500,000 X 5 = $12,500,00). Now that we know that we will pass on *that much* to them, it seems logical that we will need to care more about where our children go to school; what friends they spend time with; who they will marry; and the expectations that we should place on them and their children to make sure they do better than we did, and will continue to grow the legacy that we bequeathed to them.

Use the *Financial Family Tree* to discuss intergenerational financial planning at your upcoming family reunions and holiday visits. Remember that Proverbs 13:22 says, "A good man leaves an inheritance for his children's children." When children are raised with legacy in mind, their conditioning and capacity to achieve, and their orientation toward the future will be different.

Wills and Trusts

Your will is the final declaration of how your assets and family (e.g., guardianship of minors) are to be treated after your death. It is your way to continue to exercise control from the grave, ensure that your estate is created, and detail your legacy planning. As such, your will needs to be carefully thought out and must address all of the potential issues that may face your survivors. Many people want simple wills but fail to realize the importance of a well-drafted, comprehensive will.

For example—true story—a woman had a child by a drug dealer who had been in and out of prison for years. The man had never seen the child or provided support. However, a number of years later, the child and the mother were both injured in a car accident. The woman died immediately, and the child died 12 hours later. The lawyer who drafted the mother's will provided that all of her assets pass to her son at her death. The son actually held the assets for only 12 hours. Then, in accordance with state inheritance law, the drug dealer inherited his son's entire estate, including several million dollars from lawsuits resulting from the death of the woman and her child. It was a simple will, but it certainly did not do what this woman would have wanted.

With that cautionary tale in mind, your will should fulfill a number of purposes, including:

- Providing for how your assets should be disposed of at your death;
- Choosing the people who will make decisions when you are gone;
- Creating trusts for heirs who may lack the maturity or talents to manage inherited assets;
- Providing for the guardians of any minor children;
- Minimizing any state and/or federal estate taxes;
- Reducing heirs' state and/or federal income taxes; and
- Minimizing the sources of potential conflicts among your family members.

It is amazing how many people either do not have a will or do not know that their prior will has been revoked. I personally took way too long to get my will in order, believing that I always had time to get it done. I'm simply saying that the failure to have a will may result in significant problems and have devastating effects on those you love and want to protect most. In addition to your will, make sure that your beneficiary designations are up to date. For example, have you taken your ex-spouse off your retirement plan or life insurance policy? Do you have more children who you need to add to those documents?

Along with your will, you should prepare two other documents of utmost importance:

Living Will

A living will is a document explaining whether or not you want to be kept alive on hospital life support systems if you fall terminally ill and would die shortly without life support, or devolve into an irreversible coma or persistent vegetative state. It can provide direction and reduce ambiguity during a difficult time by spelling out your end-of-life wishes regarding the use of feeding tubes, resuscitation, and other procedures that might be needed to prolong your life. Ultimately, having a living will in place should comfort your loved ones and reduce the chances that they will be divided over whether additional measures should be taken to keep you alive. Unlike your last will and testament, the living will has nothing to do with property division after your death.

Healthcare Proxy

This document is sometimes called a "durable power of attorney for healthcare." You appoint someone and grant him or her the authority to make ongoing medical decisions on your behalf in the event you are unable to express your medical-treatment preferences. Most commonly, this situation occurs because you have fallen unconscious, or legally lack the mental capacity to make your own decisions.

Lastly, I want to briefly define a "trust" in this planning conversation. It's is a fiduciary arrangement that allows a third party, or trustee, to hold assets on behalf of a beneficiary or beneficiaries. It allows you to:

- **Control your wealth**—You can specify the terms of precisely when and to whom distributions may be made.
- **Protect your legacy**—You can help protect your estate from your heirs' creditors, or former spouses. (This is the situation we discussed earlier, which my parents were concerned about).
- **Maintain privacy and save on fees and taxes**—You can save on estate and income taxes, avoid probate costs (attorney and executor fees), maintain privacy, and avoid estate-administration delays.

This book is primarily about the untold secrets of wealth creation, but wealth *protection* is equally important. To make money, then to lose it; blow it; have it seized, unnecessarily taxed, or transferred to some unintended or undeserving persons; or not to be remembered as the gift benefactor and legacy creator will ultimately be considered a waste of time and effort. Please be smart as you incorporate each Untold Rule, and engage credible financial and estate-planning assistance.

Private Family Foundation

Some say they don't want to leave millions to their children. And some might not have children of their own. If this is your reality, you may consider structuring a foundation in a way that positively impacts and empowers those about whom you care as part of your own lifetime legacy. We sometimes hear of an athlete or entertainer setting up a foundation in his or her name, with perhaps a scholarship or organization as the beneficiary. The secret here is *that you don't have to be rich to do the same for yourself and your family!* Let's take a quick look at another thing that those with wealth do.

A private family foundation is a vehicle designed to allow families to achieve their philanthropic goals in a tax-efficient manner, where funds typically come from members of a single family. At least one family member must continue to serve as an officer or board member of the foundation, and as the primary donor. Family foundations come in all sizes. Some are enormous and work on an international scale, such as the Bill & Melinda Gates Foundation, while others are small and focused on a single issue or a particular location.

A family foundation has an initial board of directors, which typically includes the family patriarch and/or matriarch. Subsequent or additional board members usually consist of family members or close personal advisors who are familiar with the founders' goals and aspirations for the foundation. When established, a private family foundation is funded with cash, appreciated securities, or other assets. The foundation then reinvests these assets to fit the investment goals set forth by the board. It then uses the investment income and appreciated assets to make future donations or grants to charities approved by the board.

There are several primary benefits to having family members on the foundation board. Mainly, it gives the foundation a high level of control over its investment assets and its charitable giving. A secondary, but equally important, benefit of the private family foundation is that it serves as a training ground for younger family members in charitable giving, handling money, choosing investments, articulating family values, and managing intra-family relations. The tax benefits include income and estate tax benefits in one vehicle.

Setting up private family foundations and administering them is complex. I advise that you consult both an experienced certified public accountant (CPA) and an estate lawyer.

Passing Property Within the Family

Real estate is another family asset that you need to protect, especially in neighborhoods undergoing gentrification. Many in our community are sitting on gold mines but are losing out or being displaced by developers, investors, and hipsters moving in. *Gentrification* can mean different things for different people, including a revitalization and reinvestment causing a relatively sharp increase in rents and home values. To the extent that long-time residents can reap the benefits of rising home values, new small businesses, and job opportunities, gentrification is great. However, there are a few things that I want to point out from my experience of buying and living in a home in Bedford Stuyvesant ("Bed-Stuy"), Brooklyn, right before it boomed, as I felt bad for those who could not participate or didn't know how to manage the wave.

Retaining Homes in Families: This is often about financial literacy. Owners and heirs need to be prepared to handle taxes—a frequent cause of families losing property—and to efficiently transfer ownership in order to keep the property in the family. Many beneficiaries of property too often find themselves saddled with significant back taxes that went unpaid by the prior owner. Even small life insurance policies can help these receivers to avert potential seizure by tax collectors. Also, many in our communities do not have wills or haven't updated them as it pertains to the transfer of real property. I've seen this for myself, firsthand.

In 2003, my elderly neighbor died and left the house to her daughter. The sad part was that, by the time my neighbor died, her daughter had already passed away. My neighbor hadn't updated her will, and, as a result, the City of New York took over and auctioned the property. The purchaser at auction was not another African-American. This was not necessarily bad, but the house was lost to the original family, and I'm sure there were not many folks from our community who attended the auction or had the means to bid. For more information about preserving ownership and transferring properly, there are Development Zones and classes from banks and community groups to provide necessary literacy for all, at all levels.

Accessing Equity: The residential brownstones in my former neighborhood of Bed-Stuy, a predominantly African-American community, are frequently selling for over one million dollars now. However, there are families unable to tap into the increased home equity resulting from recent property appreciation on the longtime properties that they already possess.

Another one of my neighbors, in her 90s, lived there for over 40 years. Her health has deteriorated significantly over the last few years, and her granddaughter lives with her to tend to her needs. The granddaughter actually quit her government job to become a full-time caregiver, and the two now live in a four-story building, using their meager resources to pay bills and healthcare costs.

Even with the increase in property value over the years, they struggled to get a home-equity loan to help out, because there is no income to report for repayment purposes. If this is your situation, then you many consider renting either rooms or units to show income produced by the property on top of your salary. This may aid you to qualify and pay back a home-equity loan.

Of course, your credit will also be part of the qualifying process, so be sure to stay on top of that, too. Be aware: You don't necessarily have to, or continue to, live in the property. Perhaps you can rent your unit or the entire house and become a landlord. You may even be able to find another affordable accommodation or purchase another home with the money received from the home-equity loan as a down payment.

Buying Into a Gentrifying Neighborhood: Purchasing a home in Bed-Stuy now will not be cheap. A 20% down payment on a one million-dollar brownstone will set you back $200,000. Most average workers don't have $200,000 in liquid cash, and they won't save that in a lifetime for a down payment.

To obtain the necessary lump sum, many of the new purchasers, who are not Black, rely on family money for assistance. Much of that has been afforded to them from the proceeds of life insurance from parents and grandparents—yet another reason why owning significant life insurance begets more wealth, which, as you see, can be used to purchase a desired property in a burgeoning neighborhood.

Another great idea for buying in is to rent the upstairs unit of a property owned by an elderly couple. By doing so, you can get to know them and express your ownership intentions, now or in the future. You may offer to purchase the brownstone and then lease the first floor back to them, so that they don't actually have to move out. Also, like we've seen with other cultures, you can possibly pool resources together with friends or family for a down payment, and one group could live on the top two floors and the other on the bottom two. This way, you could continue to save over time and/or tap the equity for the down payment of another house.

IF WE EVER COME TOGETHER: MILLION-DOLLAR-ME ACTION STEP

Map out your family plan and create your own *Financial Family Tree.* Think about how you will empower at least three generations. Don't keep it a secret. Compare notes and encourage each other. Make it a topic of conversation for the family reunion.

Do you have a will and trust, living will, and healthcare proxy? Do an accounting of the people in your life, your businesses, and the causes that are important to you—and who you want to leave a legacy for. Be sure to also check that your selection of beneficiaries is up to date on all of your documents.

RULE #7. A RISING TIDE LIFTS ALL BOATS

SO FAR, THIS book has shared some of the best-kept secrets for navigating individual paths to wealth and explained how doing so will eradicate poverty and grow our banks, businesses, and institutions, while creating the pride, hope, jobs, and prosperity that our community needs. Now it's time to discuss ways for individuals to get connected and apply strategies that have a greater collective impact on our wealth building.

This remedial effort won't be driven by a single product or guided by one company or initiative. Only the collaboration of leaders and determined believers within our community—who bring their individual strengths, talents, and abilities together—will ensure sustainable change. We will need to highlight and support activities, programs, and groups that are already doing their part—and having economic influence and success.

Likewise, we need to divorce ourselves from activities and mindsets that undermine our efforts and proliferate negative outcomes. In doing so, we will be able to generate even greater social, political, and economic gains. There is an African proverb: *If you want to go fast, go alone. If you*

> IF YOU WANT TO GO FAST, GO ALONE. IF YOU WANT TO GO FAR, GO TOGETHER.

want to go far, go together. The strength needed for us to go far requires the assembly of a "pack" that believes in being strategic, accountable, and financially supportive of one another.

This chapter will detail the component parts that will be the driving forces and economic engines of the *Close the Wealth Gap Movement.* These components lay the foundation for this multidimensional effort. We can and must leverage our collective $1.2 trillion of earned income; our existing wealth, assets, and equity; and our ability to further borrow, influence and collaborate to achieve more.

From this collective *Close the Wealth Gap* mindset, we can scale progress and results, and transform our local action plans into a national movement focused on change at the highest levels. Doing so will rival the process and potency of the Civil Rights Movement. This is our time. This is our fight. This is our moment to propel the advancement that Dr. King fought and died for.

1. CONNECTED—WITH PRIDE, PASSION, PURPOSE, AND A PLAN

I hold dear, and repeat often when lecturing, a great saying of Rev. Willie Barrow, the powerful Chicago civil rights activist, which I quoted at the start of this book: "We are not so much divided, as we are disconnected." When I say this, I'm referring to the many ambassadors and advocates for change in our community. I often travel throughout this country, particularly for business. When I do so, I see that many community-based folks are doing great things, but are typically working separately.

Many individuals and organizations actually balk at the idea of working together because they are still trapped in a mentality that feeds off of fear and doubt. Some of us hold firm to the idea that: *More for them means less for me,* or *Success for them means failure for me.* They do not understand that it's about equity and parity—where *both* parties benefit—not polarity, where the *only* way to have a gain for one is through a loss for the other. The old saying, "*A rising tide lifts all boats*" is the perfect illustration of the direction needed for our community. When one succeeds, and then uses that success to empower and create opportunities for others, we all win. Your success is my success.

Building and maintaining unity—familial, community, national, and racial—will allow us to focus on cooperative economics and economic self-reliance. We know this to be true and must endeavor to make it a priority. No one outside of our community is going to fix the plague of poverty, crime, broken homes, and broken dreams. As the saying goes: *No one is going to do more for us than we are willing to do for ourselves.*

While some of us are content to just sit and wait, while being distracted by false symbols of wealth or replicating poor habits, this lack of proactivity and discipline is pulling the ownership of real assets and access to true wealth and power out from under us. In addition, economic resources are being siphoned from some of us by outsiders who view our communities as nothing more than places ripe for harvest.

For decades, the Kwanzaa principles of Umoja ("unity") and Ujamaa ("cooperative economics") have told us to stay focused and united. Manifesting unity and cooperative economics will allow us to write checks, not just work for checks written by others. Within the context of the larger American society, this means having a seat at the table.

Understand that what I am espousing isn't a call for radical behavior, racial superiority, or racial exclusion. Instead, we are advocating for our deliberate inclusion—working alongside everything and everyone already prospering in the larger society. We must absolutely work with all people and cultures across the world to manifest and maximize good for our community.

Enhancing our economic strength enables us to become viable, respected, contributing players in the contexts of business, politics, and societal issues. It will create a community in which we don't want or need handouts. It will also make us accountable for our success and responsible for the actions that lead to our failure. Either way, we embrace the belief that we truly are masters of our own destiny.

As masters, we can be more conscientious of our spending. Let's bank, buy, invest, advocate, and support each other with a Black-first focus. Other cultures do it. We see it clearly in the Asian and Jewish communities around us. In those cultures, cooperative economics is the expectation, akin to a community mandate. Moreover, it's not just the expected way, but also the respected way, to do business. In fact, such community interest and involvement is common sense. We must do the same, knowing that it will have a broad and noticeable impact now, and position us for a brighter future.

Enough is enough! The historical disadvantages, derailment, and sabotage through phenomena like redlining; abusive, deliberate subprime loans deceptively given to those of us who qualify for prime loans; and payday lenders have led to setbacks in the Black middle class that handicapped individuals and families—financially, psychologically, and socially—for generations.

Becoming united and focused as an economic group and voice, we can stand up, speak out, call foul, and demand penalties when negative issues impacting our communities arise. We can protest *and* progress simultaneously! From taking corrective legal action where necessary, to purposely redirecting our collective spending and shifting our accounts and consumer loyalty, let's make sure that we can wield influence and instill fear of consequences for mistreating, disrespecting, or taking the Black community for granted—socially, politically, and economically.

The trailblazers who came before us made sacrifices far greater than we will ever comprehend. They gave voice to multiple movements, seeking change. Silence, for them, was never an option. Yet, so many of us have become compliant with the ongoing inequity and injustice that plague our communities. Periodically, some new outrage will set our collective anger ablaze, but, given a week or two, what was once a fire weakens into embers—and is ultimately swept away as dead ash. Such complacency and fecklessness eventually lead to collusion against our interests—and whether overt or covert, the impact is the same: *Nothing. Ever. Changes.*

We don't have the luxury of being silent. The stakes are too high, and we are fighting for nothing less than the fate of the Black community. Understanding our history will instill pride; manifesting our own destiny will stir our passion; understanding all that we have to gain will fill us with a sense of purpose; and utilizing the tools for success that I'm sharing in this book will help us to plan accordingly.

WE ARE FIGHTING FOR NOTHING LESS THAN THE FATE OF THE BLACK COMMUNITY.

Keeping these ideas in mind, let's connect with each other and, with pride, passion, and purpose, commit to an action plan!

The next section will define the key components of our *Close the Wealth Gap Movement*, as well as its economic engines and driving forces.

2. THE ECONOMIC ENGINES OF OUR NEW ECONOMIC MOVEMENT

The buying power of Black America is over $1.2 trillion. Comparatively speaking, in the context of the Gross Domestic Product (GDP) of all the world's countries, the buying power of Black Americans ranks as the globe's 14th-largest economy. While this is not an apples-to-apples comparison, theoretically the economic power of the black community is representative of a small country.

The basic principles of any country are to create economic stability, sustainable development, peace, and a plan for their younger generations of citizens. Likewise, our community needs to embrace its responsibility and utilize its financial strength and resources to provide the same for its members. With the size and scale of the 46 million Black people here in America, we could literally apply the same strategic thinking to leveraging our buying power, assets, and existing wealth, to create a harmonious, safe, and thriving Black community.

At the heart of a thriving Black community would be a foundation of strong businesses and employment options to provide resources for everyone to get ahead. Since these strong businesses would be surrounded by more empowered community members, the community would become more self-sufficient and self-sustaining. To bring this vision to fruition here in our community, there are nine specific economic engines that can be implemented to supply, support, and return cash flow, as well as build wealth for the individuals and businesses.

In Diagram 22, I've highlighted nine economic engines. They depict a community-wide collaboration through a hub-and-spoke structure. At the center is the thriving community and economy, and the nine areas surrounding them feed the center and support each other.

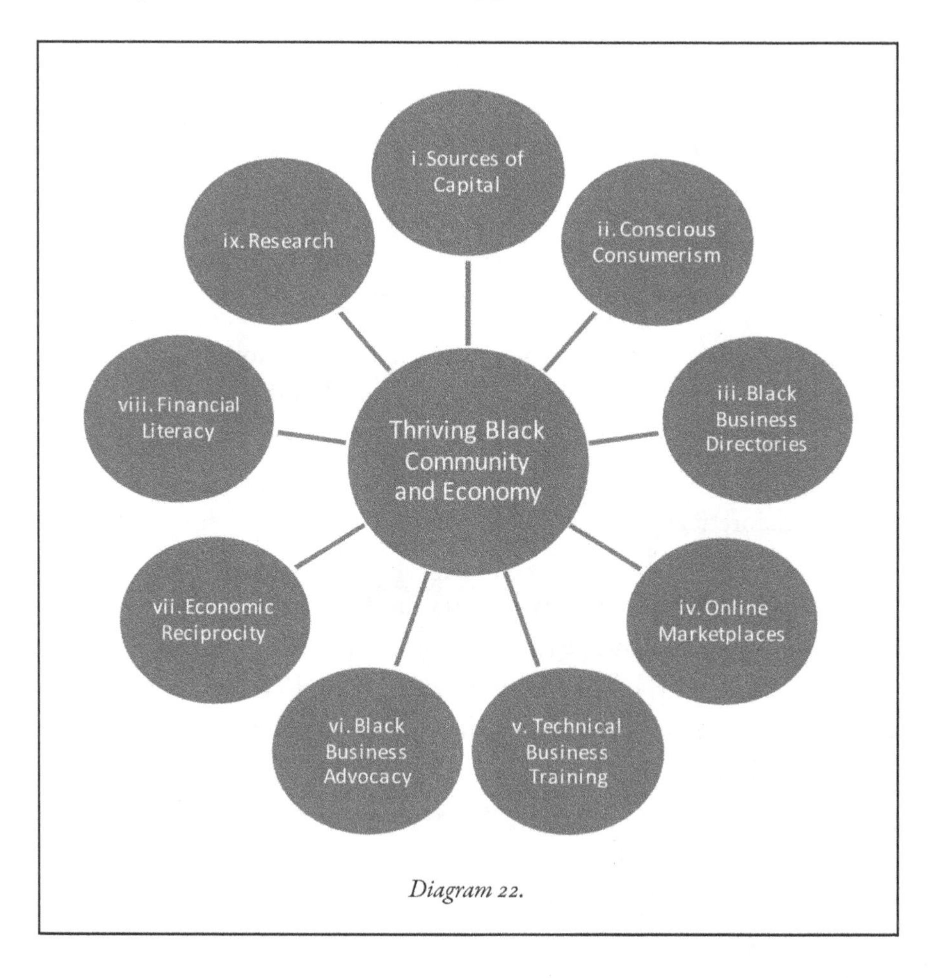

Diagram 22.

I. Sources of capital

Within the thriving Black community and economy, we can include entities that are able to manage and leverage the finances associated with our earnings, investments, real estate, equity, loans, life insurance, and so forth. Specifically, I'm referring to majority Black-owned banks, investment companies, realtors, insurance, and financial planning agencies and advisors. In addition, there are government programs for businesses and foundation grants that provide reservoirs and accessible capital sources. Some groups specifically have mandates for community reinvestment and empowerment. These companies and the community can strengthen each other through mutual support. As an example, more deposits made into community banks will allow them to, in turn, loan money to businesses that might not have received support from non-community organizations. We need to become intentional and allocate a portion of our finances to support growth in this area. I've highlighted a few such companies in the Resources section.

II. Conscious consumerism

This area of the action plan is focused on a heightened awareness about what we spend our money on, and with whom we spend it. We touched on this in previous chapters when discussing the difference between false symbols of wealth and true wealth-building practices for individuals. We must also consider duplicating these efforts on a community-wide basis. We can steer a portion of our $1.2 trillion in spending power towards patronizing our own businesses, thereby helping them to become economically viable—and eventually to thrive financially. Those businesses can then employ community members to work at their establishments, allowing them to become more productive members of society. These productive citizens can then purchase homes, send their kids to college, invest appropriately, and participate in all the other facets of healthy citizenry, such as voting, community activism, and volunteerism. The cyclical effect and impact of conscious consumerism cannot be understated. Better businesses, better employment opportunities, and better housing markets lead to better schools, investments in new business, and an influx of new residents.

III. Black business directories

This driving force sounds simple and straightforward, but it is sorely lacking. Those that exist are incomplete—hence an area of opportunity. Finding quality Black-owned businesses has been a challenge for many, and it is an easy scapegoat for not cycling our dollars. Beyond the occasional list of barbershops, beauty salons, and restaurants, we have to expand our directories to support our professionals—e.g., doctors, dentists, lawyers, accountants, and financial planners. Directories should include dealerships, franchises, contractors, employment, and entertainment services. Some successful directories are geographically focused, and some have started enhancing their sites by adding additional capabilities, such as business reviews, rankings, and comments sections that can provide listed businesses with invaluable feedback on how to grow and enhance their goods and services.

IV. Online marketplaces

An online marketplace is a type of e-commerce website where consumer transactions are processed by the marketplace operator, and then fulfilled by the participating retailers or wholesalers, like Amazon and Etsy. In general, because marketplaces aggregate products from a wide array of providers, selection is usually wider and availability is higher than in vendor-specific online retail stores. Also, prices may be more competitive. Leveraging this technology can be an area of opportunity that will allow Black businesses to collaborate online as a one-stop destination. This technology will also give Black vendors a platform to buy and sell globally, across the Diaspora. There are not many players in this realm yet that are specifically designated for the Black community, or that are Black owned—though one good, thriving example is www.webuyblack.com. It is a driving force to be considered. In the meantime, Black entrepreneurs should take advantage of the opportunity and distribution reach of existing, "mainstream" online marketplaces.

V. Technical business training and support

With over two million Black-owned businesses around the country, professional development in the workplace is vital for small and medium-sized businesses to survive and thrive. Likewise, the input of seasoned, high-quality, high-caliber business mentors can have an enormous impact, particularly for early-stage startup entrepreneurs. Training should enhance employees' skills and leadership competencies, decrease the need for supervision, ensure staff retention, improve employee morale, and enhance the company's image as both a business and an employer of choice. Workforce development is a key focus area that will allow Black businesses to survive and succeed for the second and third generations, and beyond.

VI. Black business advocacy
Advocating for Black businesses includes promoting and protecting their right to own, operate, and grow their own enterprises. However, more importantly, it's about helping them to network, position themselves for contracts, and take advantage of supplier-diversity opportunities, and supplier-diversity programs—which span the realm of public and privately owned companies, healthcare organizations, colleges and universities, and government entities—seeking to increase the participation of Minority and Women-Owned Business Enterprises ("MWBEs"). They mainly do so by setting aside a percentage of procurement opportunities for MWBEs. In addition to the compliance requirement that compels organizations to contract with MWBEs, many supplier-diversity programs also provide business training and support (e.g., bridge-loan programs, financial literacy courses, payroll assistance services, etc.) to help small MWBE owners sustain their businesses. To vie for contracts and opportunities under these programs, many businesses will need specified state and/or federal certifications. These certifications will help small minority enterprises increase new business and connect to a vast network of other entrepreneurs mandated to contract with them. As another driving force in the *Close the Wealth Gap Movement* action plan, advocacy is important, in order to get into the right circles and to gain entrance into new industries or businesses—particularly when MWBEs lack experience and connections.

VII. Economic reciprocity
The word "reciprocity" means the practice of exchanging things with others for mutual benefit. In relation to businesses in the Black com-

munity, such reciprocity can refer to the members trading goods and services with one another for profit and support. It can also refer to the expectation that large corporate entities that sell goods and services to the Black community share their gains *with* the community, in meaningful support *of* the community. This can be accomplished through the placement of advertisements into Black-owned media outlets, the creation of their own company-driven supplier diversity programs, and through the support of community reinvestment programs. Typically, multibillion-dollar industries that have a strong presence in the Black community recycle little of that money back into Black media or supplier-diversity efforts. Beauty and hair products, clothing, and alcohol, in particular, are industries that make tremendous profits from their large African-American consumer base. Hence, reciprocity must become more than just an area of the action plan. It must become an expectation: *If we spend with you, then you must invest in us.* Conversely: *If you will not invest in us, then we will not spend with you.*

VIII. Financial literacy

This is the ability to use knowledge and skill to effectively manage one's financial resources for a lifetime of financial security. We have touched on many aspects of financial awareness in this book: building, protecting, leveraging, and passing on wealth. However, there are countless other experts, blogs, editorials, videos, and programs to be considered. With 46 million people in the Black community, many of whom are in need of financial literacy, it is incumbent upon Black individuals to find programs that work for them. When it comes to the massive transformation that we are hoping to bring about, an abundance of information and resources only strengthens our community. Closing the wealth gap and creating generational legacies requires a Herculean effort. We need every soldier we can find to help in this fight, and we have to use every weapon in our arsenal.

IX. Research

The last area of focus pertains to researching and tracking the economics, financial planning, and wealth gap in the Black community. There is a need to focus not only on the current state of the wealth gap, but on the historical context, related factors, and considerations that continue to impact it. There are current studies that explore the effects of public policy on the Black community, while others have analyzed mindset, cultural habits, and personal responsibility. Many nonprofits provide statistics, via reports, charts, and videos, that are incorporated into news articles and publications. Such research and analytics are growing areas of importance to delve into and track, particularly because of our growing buying power, the future retirement needs of our aging population, and the upcoming wealth transfer from Baby Boomers. There also needs to be more study and scrutiny about the loss and raiding of Black wealth, due to social problems, racism, and discrimination. Increased knowledge and trackable metrics can aid in charting our path and monitoring the progress of the Movement. We must examine not only *what* Black Buying Power is, but also *where* it is and *what* it is doing.

These nine economic engines can support our businesses, our ongoing struggle against economic injustice, and our overall economic-empowerment focus. Alignment of these driving forces, within a comprehensive action plan, will provide an opportunity for everyone in the community to participate and proliferate. I invite everyone to analyze these nine areas, and to pick your interest and/or lane to drive in. You can help to lead the Movement, participate in it, or support it. This action plan will foster even greater pride and connectedness and rebuild and revitalize inner cities that have been left behind. Let's use our ingenuity, creativity, tenacity, and determination to further build and inspire our own. This foundation will eventually allow a shift in our focus to expand beyond economics to safety, health, justice, education, and other social reform.

I've included two case studies below of businesses that exemplify these ideas and have used their enterprises as a springboard to drive economic empowerment and build their own local, thriving Black communities. Let's learn from what is working:

3. CASE STUDIES

Case Study #1: Buy the Block, Empower the Neighborhood—The Akwaaba Way

Around 2003, when I bought a brownstone in Bedford Stuyvesant, Brooklyn, I remember being in awe of Monique Greenwood and her husband, Glenn Pogue, who had previously bought a nearby building with five commercial spaces and six apartments above. They rented the commercial spaces to local entrepreneurs. One space was a bookstore called Brownstone Books. There was also an antiques store named the Parlor Floor, and a café called Mirrors. In addition, two years earlier, they'd opened a restaurant on the corner named Akwaaba. Complementing this group of businesses was their Akwaaba Mansion, a few blocks away, where they catered to a bed-and-breakfast clientele, in four elegantly furnished rooms of an 18-room house.

In Ghana, they explained, "Akwaaba" means "welcome." Ms. Greenwood, who was editor-in-chief of *Essence* magazine at the time, and her husband had become entranced with the neighborhood when they went on a tour of historic homes 11 years prior. Ms. Greenwood was quoted in a magazine article, "First we fell in love with the houses, and then with the people who lived in the houses." The community, she said, "has everything I would ever want, except some amenities."

What transpired, as a result of her commercial-building purchase, was the opening of multiple new businesses that she owned. The amenities she provided were a source of great community pride and much media attention and caused many to flock to, and support, the companies. Shortly thereafter, numerous other small businesses and restaurants popped up, having seen an opportunity to copy and learn from what Monique and her husband had done.

Ensuing interest in the area, as a result of the overall development, and excitement, transferred into increased home sales, and property values skyrocketed. As great as that was, the greatest triumph in community empowerment was the creation of numerous new jobs that employed a majority of African-Americans from the surrounding neighborhood. The business foundation that Monique and her husband provided the community generated handsome profits, created new role models for others to emulate, and increased employment opportunities. We, too, can own our blocks, and empower our neighborhoods.

Case Study #2: Build a Local Movement and Black Business Directory App—and Rally Customers

In 2015, I had the pleasure of meeting Ajamu Webster in Kansas City, Kansas ("KC") and learning about the Buy Black Empowerment Initiative that he'd helped to start, and with which he remained intimately involved. Mr. Webster and his fellow Black community stakeholders had seen the need for economic empowerment in the KC area and had created the Buy Black Empowerment Initiative (BBEI) to educate community members about, and engage them in, supporting Black-owned businesses.

A corporate executive turned entrepreneur, Mr. Webster called his friends—corporate representatives; heads of professional, faith, and university organizations; press; small-business owners; everyday citizens; and community organizers—to action by asking them to commit to participating in BBEI. In turn, those friends called their own friends, and asked the same of them.

Then they all laid out a plan to dedicate their talents, time, and influence to buying Black. That plan included weekly meetings, the committing of time and resources, and rallying volunteers to recruit local Black businesses to join BBEI. They agreed to meet every week to grow that list of local Black businesses, and they used those meetings to plan Buy Black events and to track the spending of participants at the events. They also shared their mission and progress with the press.

As part of the initiative, they also created a free "Buy Black KC" phone app, for Android and iOS platforms, so that African-Americans could identify the Black-owned businesses near them. They also took the time to call and get to know each of the businesses listed. From their personal outreach, they were able to hear the successes, goals, concerns, and challenges of each of the business owners. Leveraging this information, they partnered with organizations and institutions to provide workshops for business-development and guidance.

In collaboration with the local Black Chamber of Commerce, they brought in featured speakers and hosted Black-business expos. They also developed a catchy branding campaign, sold T-shirts, and garnered additional local publicity and accolades. The most exciting and unique campaigns that they coordinated on a regular basis were shopping drives that featured Black-owned stores. They would rally customers to spend together, as a bloc, on a particular day, and they would post pictures of the crowds in the stores with long receipts as proof of them cycling their dollars back into local Black businesses.

This amazing Kansas City team raised awareness of quality Black-owned businesses, tracked sales growth of those operations, and encouraged the local community to monitor and direct its spending in order to make a difference. The team was committed and united as a group of passionate advocates for their business community. They also believed that, by their doing business with other African-Americans, the owners of those establishments would be compelled to help uplift the entire community through further investment and employment.

They also saw their focused buying days as a way to encourage other African-American entrepreneurs to set up shop in Black communities by letting them know that there were community members out there dedicated to supporting their businesses. One of these business owners was quoted in the local paper as saying: "I feel that, if we start empowering each other, then we can all grow. It will bring more jobs to the community, and to the neighborhood." He continued, "It helps people who can't drive all the way to the bigger stores. And, it won't cause mom and pop stores to go out of business. I feel like we as a community can only make us stronger."

Both of these case studies embody many of the driving forces that I described earlier. They were engines for growth and advocates for the concepts of working together and supporting each other. Let's follow these examples and engage with some of the other wonderful initiatives underway around the country. I've provided a list in the Resources Section at the end of the book.

4. TAKE THE 'CLOSE THE WEALTH GAP' PLEDGE—JOIN THE MOVEMENT!

When you measure where we, as Blacks, started in America some 400 years ago, we can more than celebrate the amazing perseverance we've shown and the progress we've made. The story of the Black community has always been one of collective effort, survival, unbreakable spirit, and undeniable hope.

The chapters of this book are meant to add to that story by encouraging us to: focus on economics and further disseminate some of the wealth-building tools and strategies I've shared; collectively craft a vision and action plan designed to close the racial wealth gap; start our own movements to support Black businesses and foster thriving African-American communities in our own localities; and establish a legacy to ensure that future generations are economically empowered and educated, allowing us to continue our ascension, individually and collectively.

The critical element needed to ensure the longevity of this mission-driven Movement toward economic advancement is to have everyone, first, *make it personal* for themselves and their families; and then for all of us to *get connected* to work toward collective success. With that said, I invite you now, after reading this book, to *make it personal* for yourselves by committing to the following pledge:

THE *CLOSE THE WEALTH GAP MOVEMENT* PLEDGE:

- We have one common cause: to financially empower the Black community to close the racial wealth gap and end generational poverty.
- We are driven by pride, passion, purpose, and a plan to change the financial future of Black America.

- We are focused on changing mindsets and spending habits to become wealth builders, instead of wealth spenders.
- We recognize that our expertise is rooted in financial literacy and actions that incorporate underutilized and underleveraged financial tools and strategies.
- It starts with ME. Now that I know what I know, and I know what to do, I vow to make the changes that I can!

Next, I invite you to get connected and to become involved in the Movement, in order to create, protect, leverage, and transfer intergenerational wealth, while reinvesting back into the Black community. Please consider banking, buying, investing, advocating, and supporting Black businesses. As I've mentioned repeatedly, working together to continuously cycle our dollars within our community, and supporting Black businesses, will increase the number of workers hired, and expand our wealth, impact, and influence.

Together, we can truly transform and overcome the issues that plague our community, like poverty, crime, lack of education, lack of opportunities, and hopelessness. These symptoms are the result of a deep-seated community disease—one created by unstable or non-existent community economics. Just like any disease, one can find the cure to all that ails us through an antidote—in this case, the significant infusion of economic strategies and the stability that comes from wealth building, economic empowerment, and long-term vitality.

Visit *www.closethewealthgap.com* to register. Tell me your thoughts and spread the word about your financial programs and their specific connection to the five racial wealth gap drivers that we discussed earlier in the Black Economic Empowerment section of the book. Share your stories of triumph and failure, and feel free to reach out and request additional resources from the people and programs I've highlighted throughout this book and on the website. When you sign up for our mailing list, you'll receive our quarterly newsletter and updates. Please also *like* our Facebook page (*Close the Wealth Gap Movement*) so we can stay connected—and make this Movement go viral.

Having read this book, here's what else you know: *You're a Million-Dollar Asset.* And you're one who is now equipped with *The 7 Untold Rules for Black Prosperity and Legacy* necessary to achieve sustainable, intergenerational, life- and community-transforming success!

Now is the time to act. Thank you for joining me on this journey.

Together, united, we know no bounds!

IF WE EVER COME TOGETHER: MILLION-DOLLAR-ME ACTION STEP

Identify companies, coaches, and consultants that can give you personal and professional guidance, and help you to establish your goals, and—where possible—provide support and an accountability system to help you to reach them.

And, lastly, join the *Close the Wealth Gap Movement!*

RESOURCES

EMPOWERED BUSINESSES AND CONCEPTS UNDERWAY— GET INVOLVED!

THIS SECTION FEATURES a detailed list of 24 businesses, initiatives, and leaders from around the country that are making a difference by leveraging the nine economic engines for a thriving Black community and economy that I previously shared. Clearly, this list is not all-inclusive, and there are more businesses and programs that should be listed here. I invite you to share your business or program, along with its impact, via the website www.closethewealthgap.com. I would like to feature as many of you as I can, as we build this movement together. Let's get connected and support each other!

ARIEL INVESTMENTS—(SOURCE OF CAPITAL)

Ariel Investments (Ariel) is one the largest minority-owned investment firms. Located in Chicago, Illinois, it specializes in no-load mutual funds for investment accounts, IRAs, 401(k) plans/rollovers, and college savings programs for individual investors.

In 1983, John W. Rogers, Jr., Ariel's Chairman and CEO, founded the company. Mellody Hobson has been President of the company since May

2000. It employs 88 people, with the employees and the board owning 95% of the company, and it has over $10 billion under management. Ariel wins numerous awards every year for investment performance and service. In October 2017, *Investment News* named Ariel Fund as one of the top ten performing funds since as far back as the 1987 stock market crash.

For more information, visit: *www.arielinvestments.com*

BLACK ENTERPRISE—(SOURCE OF CAPITAL, BUSINESS DIRECTORY, ADVOCACY, AND CONSCIOUS CONSUMERISM)

Black Enterprise is a business, investing, and wealth-building resource for African-Americans. Led by President & CEO Earl "Butch" Graves, Jr., Black Enterprise is a total media firm with a singular mission. It's website states: "We will educate and empower our audience to become full participants in wealth creation within the global economy." Black Enterprise affirms your aspirations and provides the tools to achieve them through their four content channels: Publishing, Digital, Broadcast, and Events.

The centerpiece of Black Enterprise's content is its 10 Wealth for Life principles. They provide relevant information to success-minded people at every stage of their financial journey: from the recent college graduate taking that first step toward financial independence; to the seasoned mid-lifer looking to maximize career options and investment opportunities; to the retiree who wants to be able to enjoy the fruits of a lifetime of hard work. All of Black Enterprise's content channels speak directly to its mantra of wealth building.

Publishing—*Black Enterprise* magazine connects, on a personal level, with African-Americans who are serious about success. Its coverage is about you—your life, your challenges, and your aspirations. Its expertise will empower you to make the best choices when it comes to building your career, your business and, ultimately, your wealth. For four decades it's shown how best to earn and manage money.

Digital—Achieving "wealth for life" isn't a once-a-month task; it requires day-to-day, moment-to-moment engagement. With BlackEnterprise.com, you are always connected to breaking financial news and have direct access to exclusive Black Enterprise broadcasts, podcasts, video, and live events, as well as to a host of forums and blogs that allow direct interaction with its outstanding content team.

Broadcast—A broad spectrum of African-American entrepreneurs, corporate executives, innovators, investors, and entertainers are the centerpiece of its two nationally syndicated television programs: the *Black Enterprise Business Report,* a fast-paced, half-hour financial news magazine, and *Our World with Black Enterprise,* a timely, in-depth, weekly examination of the issues and trends shaping our lives. In addition, *Women of Power* on their BETV platform provides viewers with an intimate, in-depth look into the lives of some of the world's most accomplished women.

Events—The Black Enterprise Women of Power Summit (Women of Power) is a four-day executive leadership conference, designed to prepare and embolden women executives of color to take risks, think strategically, and rise above all challenges. Women of Power is dedicated to career advancement and executive skill building, but it also focuses on the unique challenges that women of color face outside the workplace. The Black Enterprise Entrepreneurs Summit is the epicenter of dynamic, full-throttle networking and deal making. This event delivers in-demand speakers, professional connection opportunities, and first-rate seminars and workshops.

For more information, visit: *www.blackenterprise.com*

BLACK PAGES—(BUSINESS DIRECTORY, ADVOCACY, AND CONSCIOUS CONSUMERISM)

The *Black Pages* publications give exposure and visibility to minority-owned firms, especially African-American ones, as well as to Fortune® 500 companies that desire to target and reach those firms and their consumers. The *Black Pages* concept started over 30 years ago in Atlanta, Georgia. Today, it publishes in 30 cities and metropolitan areas throughout the United States.

The *Black Pages'* mission is to encourage, support, and facilitate economic empowerment of the African-American community through the development of a strategic, local business network, educational initiatives, and communication ventures. The *Black Pages South* also hosts the Black Expo South, a three-day event in Columbia, Charleston, and Greenville, South Carolina, and Jacksonville, Florida, attracting over 800 exhibitors and 85,000 visitors.

For more information, visit: *http://blackpagessouth.com*

BLACKMAN AND ASSOCIATES—(FRANCHISE OWNERSHIP, BLACK BUSINESS ADVOCACY, AND TRAINING)

There are thousands of franchise opportunities for entrepreneurs seeking a proven brand concept. The top franchise industry is fast food, with McDonald's leading the pack. However, there are other hot brands out there, based on franchisee needs and niche markets. According to the Washington, DC–based industry trade group, International Franchise Association, roughly 825,000 franchise businesses, across 300 different business categories, provide nearly 18 million jobs and contribute over $2.1 trillion to the economy.

Blackman and Associates is a franchise-consulting firm that provides franchise advisory and acquisition services for individuals and companies. *Blackman and Associates* identifies the most viable and lucrative franchise opportunities for its clients—both startups and those who already own other franchises. The firm provides market research, marketing strategies, business-plan development, franchise management, recruitment, deal searches, acquisition of both debt and equity financing, and strategic franchise-growth planning.

Owned by CEO Kevin Hicks—the first Black Denny's franchisee—the firm's stated mission is to help more Black entrepreneurs realize the wealth and job-building benefits of franchise ownership and increase the number of Black influencers among the most successful franchise chains.

For more information, visit: *www.blackmanandassoc.com*

BME COMMUNITY—(BLACK BUSINESS ADVOCACY, AND FINANCIAL LITERACY)

BMe Community ("BMe") is a real-world social and membership network of inspired Black men, and thousands of their families and friends from different walks of life, who share a common belief in building upon assets, rather than dwelling upon deficits. Founder and CEO Trabian Shorters has a long history of creating and running innovative networks for the public good. The BMe Community continues his work by providing its members with a positive environment, inspiring stories, and the ability to connect with diverse, inspired people who are committed to the public good in a variety of ways.

The BMe Community also provides its members with a news service, a Web tool to create and cross-promote events, and access to information for improving health, building wealth, acquiring know-how, and expanding their networks. Each year, BMe identifies exemplary local Black men from a broad number of stations in life, and names them "BMe Leaders"—an honor that includes expanded networking opportunities, funding, and considerable public recognition.

Launched in July 2013, the BMe Community has funded nearly 200 BMe Leaders who have helped over two million of their neighbors in Akron, Baltimore, Detroit, Miami, Philadelphia, and Pittsburgh. Its programs and staff have received national and international acclaim. Influencers at some of the nation's leading African-American organizations have requested their revolutionary "Asset-Framing" training and talks. BMe has over 40,000 members and followers.

For more information, visit: *http://www.bmecommunity.org/*

DFREE®—(FINANCIAL LITERACY AND CONSCIOUS CONSUMERISM)

The global financial freedom movement dfree® is empowering organizations and individuals to lead richer lives by improving how they think about, and manage, their money. Its goal is to help African-Americans pay down $1 billion in debt by the year 2020. The Billion Dollar Challenge (BDC) is the marquee initiative of dfree®. Through the challenge, participants have free tools and an interactive tracking system for paying down their debt. Most join the initiative's undertaking to create financial freedom and economic strength in the African-American community.

BDC participants are enrolled as individuals, as well as groups. Right now, there are more than 60 Chapters of Delta Sigma Theta Sorority, Incorporated enrolled in the Billion Dollar Challenge. To date, these Delta chapters have collectively paid down more than $1 million in debt. Author and SiriusXM radio host Karen Hunter also recently started a BDC group, contributing to the more than 5,000 people currently participating in the Billion Dollar Challenge.

Founded in 2005, the dfree® financial freedom movement is a transformational lifestyle movement that promotes financial freedom through value-based principles and practical approaches to financial management. Also, dfree® addresses the cultural, psychological and spiritual influences on financial wellness. Founder Rev. Dr. DeForest B. "Buster" Soaries, Jr. is an active agent for change. He is the Senior Pastor of First Baptist Church of Lincoln Gardens in Somerset, New Jersey, and former New Jersey Secretary of State. Soaries is also the author of *Dfree: Breaking Free from Financial Slavery,* which inspired the formation of the dfree® program, and of *Say Yes to No Debt: 12 Steps to Financial Freedom.*

The Billion Dollar Challenge (BDC) is a strategy with a direct effect on the growing and widely discussed wealth gap in America. While recent studies suggest that African-American households will have a "net income of $0 by 2053," Soaries knows otherwise:

> *This forecast can be changed. We can redefine the economic state of the African-American community by taking action right now. If 125,000 people pay down the average $8,000 of household debt, $1 billion of debt will be eradicated. If those same people shift their former credit card payments to buying a $100,000 life insurance policy, we will be able to see an eradication of the estimated $100,000 wealth gap that exists between African-Americans and White Americans. That is why I am so passionate about this challenge. We do not have to accept our current state of economic affairs, nor do we have to transfer it to future generations.*

For more information, visit: *www.billiondollarpaydown.com*

FINANCIAL JUNETEENTH—(FINANCIAL LITERACY AND BLACK BUSINESS ADVOCACY)

Financial Juneteenth is a website and information hub that aims to empower Black wealth creation. It does this by providing breaking news, education, and company information within the African-American space. Led by CEO Dr. Boyce Watkins, it also manages Financial Juneteenth University, a resource where you can learn from other Black entrepreneurs who've created real businesses that make real money. According to its website, "These are actual business people who not only understand how to monetize their businesses, they also know what it's like to be Black in business. So, unlike people who tell you pie-in-the-sky stories about how their father helped them get a million-dollar bank loan to start their first company, these are down-to-earth fellow soldiers in the struggle who can actually explain how they worked to get what they needed, in order to be successful."

For more information, visit: *http://financialjuneteenth.com/*

FRASERNET, INC., POWERNETWORKING CONFERENCE—(SOURCE OF CAPITAL, FINANCIAL LITERACY, AND BLACK BUSINESS ADVOCACY)

The FraserNet, Inc., PowerNetworking Conference (PNC) hosts top global experts whose attention are focused on financial literacy, business development, and wealth building through personal "subject matter" excellence, effective networking, and collaboration in the Black community.

"Financial illiteracy is an American problem according to the *Wall Street Journal*, but it is 10 times greater in Black America," explains Dr. George Fraser, President and CEO of FraserNet, Inc. "All the studies, surveys and statistics predict that if nothing changes within our community, we will be financially destitute and enslaved by 2053." He adds, "Thus, we must effectively and aggressively address financial illiteracy and building million-dollar businesses in Black America."

During its 2018 conference, Fraser launched the national, faith-based WINDS Wealth Building Centers and Curriculum, with the goal of 10,000+ centers up and running by 2028. Fraser explained that the curriculum will focus on a mindset shift of "instant gratification to delayed gratification," with its four pillars for the inter-generational wealth transfer: proper management of accumulated wealth, real estate, business development, and proper insurance.

The PowerNetworking Conference is widely recognized as America's largest, continuously held conference in the world for Black executives, business professionals, and entrepreneurs. The PNC typically draws more than 1,200 attendees from around the world. The PNC was named one of the 5 'Can't Miss' Conferences for Entrepreneurs in 2015, in America, by *Forbes* magazine. Since its inception, the PNC has produced over $750 million in new business startups and deal flow, and it has held 16 conferences across the United States.

For more information, visit: *www.powernetworkingconference.com*

MONEYWISE WITH KELVIN BOSTON AND MONEYWISE TV—(FINANCIAL LITERACY AND CONSCIOUS CONSUMERISM)

Moneywise with Kelvin Boston is the nation's first and longest running multicultural financial television program. Formerly *The Color Of Money with Kelvin Boston*, the program premiered on public television stations in 1990. Today, *Moneywise with Kelvin Boston* continues to "empower viewers with useful and easy-to-understand financial information." The program features engaging panel discussions, enlightening documentaries, and inspiring stories about Americans from diverse backgrounds.

Moneywise TV is a financial network set to debut in 2018. It's designed to distribute financial wellness content on public TV stations, such as, Comcast VOD, Frontier VOD, Roku, Amazon Fire TV, Apple TV, iOS Mobile, Android Mobile, and on 56% of Smart TVs in the U.S.

For more information, visit: *www.moneywise.tv*

NATIONAL ASSOCIATION OF BLACK HOTEL OWNERS, OPERATORS, AND DEVELOPERS (NABHOOD)—(SOURCE OF CAPITAL, BLACK BUSINESS ADVOCACY, TECHNICAL BUSINESS TRAINING)

NABHOOD's primary goal is to increase the number of African-Americans developing, managing, operating, and owning hotels, and to increase vendor opportunities and executive-level jobs for minorities, thereby creating wealth within the African-American community. Andy Ingraham is the President and CEO of the organization, which also provides employment and additional resources. The organization's four-day summit, the Annual International African American Hotel Ownership & Investment Summit & Trade Show, facilitates many of the aforementioned goals and trains attendees to market to minorities and to address diversity issues affecting the industry. The summit features a number of executive-level professionals from the world's leading hotel brands, who share a wealth of information needed for success.

For more information, visit: *www.nabhood.net*

NATIONAL ASSOCIATION OF REAL-ESTATE BROKERS (NAREB)—TWO MILLION NEW BLACK HOMEOWNERS PROGRAM (2MN5)—(SOURCES OF CAPITAL, ADVOCACY AND FINANCIAL LITERACY)

The National Association of Real Estate Brokers (NAREB) was formed in 1947 and has 90 chapters located nationwide. With Jeffrey Hicks as its current President, NAREB is taking the lead to rebuild Black wealth by working to increase homeownership among Black Americans by two million households in five years.

The 2MN5 Program is one of NAREB's solutions cited in its semi-annual report titled, *The State of Housing in Black America* (SHIBA)®, with short- and long-term objectives to eliminate the racial wealth gap and the current disparity in homeownership in the United States (42% Black vs. 71% White, for the latter).

The Program includes the following activities:

- Advocacy for Black homeownership, with public and private sector leaders at the local, state, and federal levels;
- Advertising and marketing to Black consumers on the benefits of Black homeownership;
- Advocating for access to credit and for the change of regulatory policies and laws that will support increased Black homeownership;
- Action-based community outreach that raises awareness of the important role that homeownership plays in closing the wealth gap in the Black community;
- Neighborhood and community-development projects that foster homeownership;

- Advocacy and leadership-development training for NAREB local leaders, and for other community and neighborhood stakeholders;
- Business-development training and technical assistance for Black entrepreneurs through NAREB's Share the Wealth Series and NAREB University; and
- Events and programs promoting engagement of Black realtors, mortgage brokers, appraisers, banks and attorneys.

Progress toward its goal of 2 million more homeowners will be measured through a database management system that will track and capture sales activities across the country. Both NAREB members and participating lenders will have access to the system.

For more information, visit: *www.nareb.com/2mn5*

NATIONAL NEWSPAPER PUBLISHERS ASSOCIATION—(ADVOCACY, FINANCIAL LITERACY, AND CONSCIOUS CONSUMERISM)

National Newspaper Publishers Association ("NNPA") is a trade association of the more than 200 African-American–owned community newspapers from across the United States, led by President and CEO Dr. Benjamin F. Chavis, Jr., a global business leader, educator, and long-time civil rights activist. Since its founding over 75 years ago, NNPA has consistently been the voice of the Black community, and an incubator for news that makes history and impacts our country.

As the largest and most influential Black–owned media resource in America, NNPA delivers news, information, and commentary to over 20 million people each week. It is committed to showcasing the work of NNPA-member publications, and to telling the untold stories of the Black community in the United States and the African Diaspora.

Americans from all backgrounds seek news from the Black perspective from NNPA-member newspapers throughout the country. With the U.S. now numbering among the most diverse countries in the world, America's

Black press is more relevant than ever. However, competitors to Black-oriented media outlets and press are strong, and other outlets have seized most of the Black community's attention. Black owned newspapers and magazines—once the leading marketing and advertising arm for Black owned businesses—are suffering from a lack of advertising revenue, and subscription rates dying off.

The Black media's economic challenges mirror those of other historic Black institutions and of Black businesses in general. NNPA is the leading advocacy group for these publishers and institutions, leading campaigns designed to drive more support to its members—particularly from Black readers and consumers, as well as from mainstream brands and retailers that thrive off of the Black consumer dollar. Black entrepreneurs, professionals, and partners to the Black community have a duty to engage and advocate for Black–owned media outlets.

For more information, visit: *www.blackpressusa.com/*

ONE THOUSAND CHURCHES CONNECTED (OTCC)—(FINANCIAL LITERACY, BLACK BUSINESS ADVOCACY, AND CONSCIOUS CONSUMERISM)

The Citizenship Education Fund implemented One Thousand Churches Connected, in partnership with the Rainbow PUSH Coalition. PUSH Coalition Founder and President Reverend Jesse L. Jackson, Sr.—one of America's foremost civil rights, religious, and political figures—heads both organizations. Reinforcing the best traditions of the church as the center of family and community life, the mission of OTCC is to assist our churches to become redeeming forces for progressive change in the areas of economic justice, public policy, social justice, civil rights, and peace.

A major thrust of the One Thousand Churches Connected program is economic literacy and financial responsibility for churches and their members. For many workers, the burden of personal debt prevents them from becoming homeowners and from holding more powerful positions in society. Rising costs (in living expenses, health care, child-care, and education) and stagnant or diminishing incomes (e.g., downsizing, layoffs, and salary cuts) encourage people to carry large amounts of personal debt and have stifled the vitality and growth of many communities across the country.

Overuse of credit cards and other unhealthy financial practices have compounded the problem. In response, OTCC facilitates a financial literacy program to deliver a message of economic responsibility through the church and promotes economic opportunity through shared economic security and empowerment. Member churches are taught to establish economic independence through debt elimination and long-term financial planning. Member churches may take advantage of the following four training modules to implement each congregation's financial ministry:

- Module I: Debt & Consumer Credit Education
- Module II: Home Ownership
- Module III: Investment Basics & Insurance Education
- Module IV: Technology as a Resource

For more information, visit: *http://1000churches.com/*

ONEUNITED BANK—(SOURCE OF CAPITAL AND FINANCIAL LITERACY)

On July 8, 2016, hip hop artist Killer Mike phoned in to a town hall meeting being broadcast on MTV and BET. The politically conscious rapper called for one million Black people to deposit $100 each into a Black bank. It worked. The hashtag #BankBlack took off across Twitter, and officially became a movement.

One week later, Black people across the country had moved at least $1 million into Black banks. Perhaps no bank benefited more than America's largest Black-owned bank: Boston-based OneUnited Bank, headed by President and Chief Operating Officer Teri Williams, who is responsible for the implementation of its strategic initiatives, as well as for its day-to-day operations.

OneUnited noticed a huge influx of new accounts after #BankBlack began trending on social media platforms, boosting the financial institution's assets, which had only been $655 million at the time. OneUnited has always been aware of the power of collective Black community action. Instead of casting itself as a bank that just happens to be Black owned, it has always wanted the world to know that it is unapologetically Black, focusing on economic empowerment for the Black community since its inception.

OneUnited offers and services mortgage loans, stressing the importance of wealth building to its customer base. The bank also holds workshops and financial-literacy seminars that highlight Black economic equality. Its credit-building products are geared toward empowering its Black customer base with the tools for long-term financial success.

Black-owned banks have the same products, infrastructure, technology, and accessibility as their White counterparts. For example, in addition to savings and checking accounts, OneUnited offers the same mortgage lending, commercial-real-estate loans, business-deposit accounts, and online banking that consumers have come to rely on from larger, White-owned banks.

For more information, visit: www.oneunited.com

For a list of additional Black-owned banks and similar programs, including legislative and regulatory initiatives, visit the National Bankers Association. Chairman and CEO of City National Bank of New Jersey, Preston Pinkett, III, is currently Chairman of this iconic and historic organization: *www.nationalbankers.org/*. You can also conduct a social media search using the hashtag #BankBlack.

OPERATION HOPE—(FINANCIAL LITERACY, TECHNICAL BUSINESS TRAINING, AND SOURCE OF CAPITAL)

Operation HOPE, Inc. ("HOPE") is an American nonprofit organization, and the leading global provider of *financial-dignity* education and economic empowerment programs for low- or moderate-income individuals and families in underserved communities. HOPE serves three core constituencies: young people in underserved schools, low-income adults in underserved communities, and families who have been affected by either natural or human-made disasters.

HOPE's mission is to expand economic opportunity in underserved communities through financial education and empowerment, by offering programs that create more financial stakeholders and stable communities. It converts customers of check-cashing establishments into banking customers, renters into homeowners, small-business dreamers into small-business owners, and minimum-wage workers into living-wage workers. The overarching vision is financial inclusion and financial literacy leading to long-term financial dignity for all.

Operation HOPE is a membership organization composed of leading organizations and individuals from government, community, and the private sector. Andrew Young, former Mayor of Atlanta and former U.S. Ambassador, is the organization's global spokesman. John Hope Bryant is Chairman.

Since its inception in 1992, HOPE has served more than 2.5 million people. In addition, it has directed more than $1.8 billion in private capital to America's low-wealth communities, maintaining a growing army of 22,000 HOPE Corps volunteers, and currently serving more than 300 U.S. cities, as well as South Africa, Saudi Arabia, Morocco, and the United Arab Emirates.

For more information, visit: *www.operationhope.org*

THE EMPOWERMENT EXPERIMENT FOUNDATION—(CONSCIOUS CONSUMERISM, ADVOCACY, AND RECIPROCITY)

Author, activist and Black business advocate, Maggie Anderson, is head of The Empowerment Experiment Foundation (EEF), and one of leading spokespersons in the conscious consumerism space. Maggie, and her husband, John, garnered national attention for their year-long experiment to purchase and patronize only Black-owned businesses for goods, services, and professional needs for their family.

In doing so, their intention was to: debunk the myth that quality Black-owned businesses do not exist for every area of life; spotlight the need to spend dollars with these businesses to ensure their success; and to inspire more economic solidarity in the Black community, especially among other educated middle- and upper-class professionals and suburbanites like themselves.

The journey was documented in Maggie's critically acclaimed book, *Our Black Year: One Family's Quest to Buy Black in America's Racially Divided Economy.* The book also examined the commercial exploitation of Black neighborhoods and explored the reasons why Black businesses have lagged behind others in every measure of success. In interviews, and in the book, the Andersons argue that the social crises that disproportionately impact Black people and underserved Black neighborhoods could be countered through what they call "conscious consumerism."

Following the family's year of targeted spending, the EEF partnered with Northwestern University's Kellogg Graduate School of Management to use their collective activities and receipts to analyze and prove economic leakage in the Black community, and the potential impact of self-help economics and conscious consumerism on a mass scale. The analysis resulted in a landmark study, proving that **close to one-million new American jobs could be created if African-American consumers, with household incomes of $75,000 or more, purposely increased their spending with Black-owned businesses from the current rate of 3% of their disposable incomes, to 10%.**

This would encompass businesses big and small, including restaurants, dry cleaners, mechanics, doctors, and dentists. According to this study, which EEF co-authored with Northwestern's business school, as a result of such intentional spending, demand for products and services from Black businesses would both create a million new jobs due to increased demand for their products and services. Increased revenue would also expand their ability to hire workers.

Maggie is now on a mission to build awareness and to help consumers recognize their opportunity to contribute to her bold objective. Her motto and reminder to create a million jobs is: *3 to 10—what's your spend?* She travels from city to city to increase consumer demand, corporate engagement, and government contracts. She showcases Black-owned businesses, and advocates within large companies for the inclusion of Black firms in their supply chains, the stocking of products from Black companies, and additional engagement with Black franchisees, suppliers, dealers, and vendors.

Maggie's personal story and exemplary commitment have been tied to real data, metrics, quantifiable results, and true impact. Commitment to initiatives like this one can inspire consumers, community partners, and corporations to come together to support quality businesses, thereby delivering jobs, wealth, and role models to struggling communities.

For more information, visit: *www.authormaggieanderson.com*

BLACK FRIDAY: WHAT LEGACY WILL YOU LEAVE?— (RESEARCH, TRACKING, AND ADVOCACY)

The documentary, *Black Friday,* by Director and Producer Ric Mathis, takes an in-depth look at the spending habits of African-Americans. It chronicles the financial miseducation of many African-Americans and explores the economic pitfalls that continue to derail the progress of the community at large. In an effort to heighten community economic awareness and financial responsibility, the film presents solutions on how to better manage the $1.2 trillion that leaves the hands of African-Americans, and their communities, annually. In addition, it champions the importance of leaving a financial and ethical legacy for the next generation.

For more information, visit: *www.blackfridayfilmseries.com*

THE GRIFFIN FIRM, PLLC—(FINANCIAL LITERACY AND SOURCE OF CAPITAL)

The Griffin Firm, PLLC, is a law firm committed to economic empowerment through strategic planning, with a primary focus on intergenerational wealth transfer through estate and succession planning. It takes a comprehensive approach to creating a legacy through estate planning that supports its clients' values, while protecting their assets.

According to its website, The Griffin Firm will assist you in answering three questions: *What happens when you die? What happens when you can't manage your affairs? What is the legacy that you want to leave?* It specializes in healthcare proxy, durable power of attorney, trusts, and wills. It works with individuals, families, and businesses to strategically plan for wealth creation and transfer in order to secure and benefit multiple generations.

For more information, visit: *www.yourestateplanningattorney.com*

THE U.S. BLACK CHAMBERS, INC.—(SOURCE OF CAPITAL, BLACK BUSINESS DIRECTORY, ADVOCACY, AND TRAINING)

The U.S. Black Chambers, Inc. (USBC) is a leading voice for Black businesses, entrepreneurs, and professionals. Headquartered in Washington, D.C., it is a rapidly growing economic development organization, led by President and CEO Ron Busby, Sr. It supports 123 chapters in 29 states and represents 265,000 members. USBC advocates increasing economic parity for Black businesses by focusing on five key areas:

- **Advocacy:** Through affiliate chambers, it offers a broad range of programming to start, sustain, and enable succession planning for its members.
- **Access to Capital:** It has a strategic partnership with New Orleans–based Liberty Bank (part of the #BankBlack movement), and offers banking and lending, business credit cards, and SBA-guaranteed business loans.
- **Contracting:** It works with federal agencies and major corporations to address two key impediments to Black businesses achieving full participation: Difficulty in sourcing diverse vendors for procurement; and a lack of size and scale for small minority businesses.
- **Entrepreneurial Training:** USBC has partnered with the University of Phoenix to provide a 15-week course, focusing on contracts, business development, access to capital, and other executive-education topics essential to competing successfully.
- **Chamber Development:** Chamber leaders and boards of directors can receive world-class training and development designed to hone their business and managerial skills across a wide range of topics.

For more information, visit: *www.blackchambers.org*

WEBUYBLACK.COM—(ONLINE MARKETPLACE AND ECONOMIC RECIPROCITY)

WeBuyBlack.com is reportedly the largest online marketplace for Black (African-American and those of African descent) businesses and individual sellers. Vendors may register to sell their products to a diverse, open, and international market. Howard University Alumnus Shareef Abdul-Malik created Webuyblack.com in his senior year (2014). The site was launched for public purchases on June 19, 2015, which marked the 150th anniversary of Juneteenth.

On October 21, 2015, Webuyblack.com launched a campaign to raise $30,000 in 30 days to build a more efficient website. Not only did it reach its goal, but it also surpassed it by several thousand dollars. The site is in the process of being reconfigured to further enhance its security, overall features, speed, and to lower maintenance.

The goals of Webuyblack.com are to: uncover creative ways to help the Black community circulate its dollars more among its own community members; allow the world to find and purchase the beautiful products of the African diaspora; to position Black businesses to provide for their families and communities; and to enable Black businesses to contribute to the global economy.

For more information, visit: *https://webuyblack.com/*

WORLD OF MONEY—(FINANCIAL LITERACY)

CEO Sabrina Lamb founded WorldofMoney.org in 2005. It is a New York City–based 501(c)(3) nonprofit organization whose mission is to empower youth with a sound financial education. Since its inception, nearly 4,000 young people between the ages of 7 and 18, and their families, have received World of Money's 40 classroom hours of financial education and forums. This approach has steadily broken the generational cycle of poverty and changed the way youth and their parents understand their money.

Its immersive curriculum equips children with five tenets for a financially responsible and philanthropic life: learn, earn, save, invest, and donate. Its financial presenters are stellar Wall Street professionals, as well as business and legal leaders. The World of Money app provides young people with financial education, via 24 coalition partners, and is being utilized by these national, local, regional, and global organizations in places as far flung as Senegal, Ghana, South Africa, China, India, and Rwanda. World of Money has strengthened its commitment to providing children and their families with the proper financial tools and mindset.

For more information, visit: *http://worldofmoney.org/*

URBAN INSTITUTE—(RESEARCH AND TRACKING)

Why hasn't wealth inequality improved over the past 50 years? And why, in particular, has the racial wealth gap not closed? The Urban Institute has research to document and illustrate how income inequality, earnings gaps, homeownership rates, retirement savings, student loan debt, and lopsided asset-building subsidies have contributed to these growing wealth disparities.

The Urban Institute's research helps decision makers understand what's driving the gaps, who is most affected, and what policies can help to close them.

For more information, visit: *http://apps.urban.org/features/wealth-inequality-charts/*

SOURCES

Extensive Data Shows Punishing Reach of Racism for Black Boys—March 19, 2018: *https://www.nytimes.com/interactive/2018/03/19/upshot/race-class-white-and-black-men.html*

The racial wealth gap: How African-Americans have been shortchanged out of the materials to build wealth: *https://www.epi.org/blog/the-racial-wealth-gap-how-african-americans-have-been-shortchanged-out-of-the-materials-to-build-wealth/*

The Ever-Growing Gap—August 2016: *https://www.ips-dc.org/wp-content/uploads/2016/08/The-Ever-Growing-Gap-CFED_IPS-Final-2.pdf*

The Roots of the Widening Racial Wealth Gap: Explaining the Black-White Economic Divide—February 2013: *https://iasp.brandeis.edu/pdfs/Author/shapiro-thomas-m/racialwealthgapbrief.pdf*

The Roots of the Widening Wealth Gap: http://iasp.brandeis.edu/pdfs/Author/shapiro-thomas-m/racialwealthgapbrief.pdf

Expected Number of Deaths by Graduation Reunion: https://www.insure.com/life-insurance/high-school-reunion-shocker-dying-off.html

The Retirement Crisis Facing African Americans—March 9, 2017: https://www.forbes.com/sites/nextavenue/2017/03/09/the-retirement-crisis-facing-african-americans/#3a9bef904f5b

Northwestern Journal of Law and Social Policy article in the Fall of 2009, 'Ending Jim Crow Life Insurance Rates': https://scholarlycommons.law.northwestern.edu/cgi/viewcontent.cgi?referer=https://www.google.com/&httpsredir=1&article=1041&context=njlsp

Conspicuous Consumption and Race, University of Chicago, July 2008: http://faculty.chicagobooth.edu/erik.hurst/research/qje_published_version_final.pdf

All that kneeling ignores the real cause of soaring black homicides: https://nypost.com/2017/09/26/all-that-kneeling-ignores-the-real-cause-of-soaring-black-homicides/

The Big Reason Whites Are Richer Thank Blacks in America—inheritance matters a lot more than previously thought. Guess who's getting the lion's share: https://www.bloomberg.com/news/articles/2017-02-08/the-big-reason-whites-are-richer-than-blacks-in-america

Benefitspro.com African American Retirement Crisis: https://www.benefitspro.com/2017/04/04/the-african-american-retirement-crisis-how-auto-po/?slreturn=20180509094302

America Household Expenditures—Chart and year 2016: https://www.ers.usda.gov/data-products/ag-and-food-statistics-charting-the-essentials/ag-and-food-sectors-and-the-economy/

A Foolish Take: Here's how much debt the average U.S. household owes: https://www.usatoday.com/story/money/personalfinance/2017/11/18/a-foolish-take-heres-how-much-debt-the-average-us-household-owes/107651700/

Income and Poverty in the United States: 2016, Median Household Income: https://www.census.gov/content/dam/Census/library/publications/2017/demo/P60-259.pdf

EUGENE MITCHELL IS the President and CEO of E. Mitchell Enterprises, Inc., a financial consulting and services firm. Prior to starting his own company, Eugene spent nearly two decades as a Corporate Vice President and "African American Market" Manager at New York Life Insurance Company, leading over 1,500 financial professionals nationwide. He graduated from Florida International University—College of Business Administration with a degree in Finance and received his MBA from New York University's Stern School of Business. Eugene has been featured in *The New York Times, Black Enterprise,* BlackPressUSA.com, and on ABC and NPR News. He and his family live in New York. *Closing the Racial Wealth Gap: 7 Untold Rules for Black Prosperity and Legacy* is his first book.

Printed in the USA
CPSIA information can be obtained
at www.ICGtesting.com
CBHW072126310324
6099CB00003B/5